THE SOCIOLOGY OF
Organizational Change

PERGAMON
INTERNATIONAL
LIBRARY
of Science, Technology
Engineering &
Social Studies

THE SOCIOLOGY OF
Organizational Change

E A JOHNS

BSc (Econ), ACIS, AMIPM, AMBIM, Dip Ed

Principal Lecturer in Management (Behavioural Sciences)
Slough College of Technology

PERGAMON PRESS

OXFORD · NEW YORK · TORONTO
SYDNEY · BRAUNSCHWEIG

Pergamon Press Ltd., Headington Hill Hall, Oxford

Pergamon Press Inc., Maxwell House, Fairview Park, Elmsford,
New York 10523

Pergamon of Canada Ltd., 207 Queen's Quay West, Toronto 1

Pergamon Press (Aust.) Pty. Ltd., 19a Boundary Street,
Rushcutters Bay, N.S.W. 2011, Australia

Vieweg & Sohn GmbH, Burgplatz 1, Braunschweig

First edition 1973

Library of Congress Cataloging in Publication Data

Johns, Edward Alistair.
The sociology of organizational change.

Bibliography: p.
1. Organizational change. I. Title.
HD38.J54 1973   301.18′32   73–8972
ISBN 0–08–017601–1
ISBN 0–08–017602–X (flexicover)

Printed in Great Britain by A. Wheaton & Co., Exeter

To My Wife

whose talent for resisting change
is second to none

Contents

Preface

To SOCIOLOGISTS, the term "progressive" as applied to organizations seems to be synonymous with the employment of sociologists or, at the very least, the systematic application of sociology in the management of the firm. Yet, in practice, remarkably few organizations could be described as progressive in these terms. Perhaps this is because, when the chips are down, managers tend to revert to older well-established nostrums (even if their practical utility is dubious). Or perhaps sociologists themselves do not offer the kind of pragmatic advice and ready-made packages which executives would prefer to exploit.

Unfortunately (but inevitably) sociology lacks the apparent certainty and factual basis of such disciplines as engineering. The sociologist in particular can rarely make predictions of an absolute nature. His statements are expectations of probability, hedged with qualifications which diminish their value to the practitioner. Also there is the suspicion, sometimes well-founded, that the sociologist is more concerned with the happiness of the employee than with such mundane matters as profit and survival.

In this book I have tried to overcome these communication barriers. I am unashamedly in favour of economic growth, the specification and attainment of profitability targets, and entrepreneurial behaviour. Nonetheless, I believe that the sociologist has something valuable to offer in assisting organizations to achieve these aims, particularly in a highly effervescent and dynamic environment. The problems of organizational change are not new in themselves, but have become significant simply because of the accelerating pace of change itself. This book seeks to offer managers some relevant guidance on the range of methods available for handling change with least damage to themselves, their organizations, and their people.

At the same time I have attempted what many critics may well say is impossible by simultaneously supplying help to managers and sustain-

ing a respectable degree of academic impartiality and analytical detach-
ment. With these two aims in mind, the sources quoted vary from
learned journals to case-studies appearing in the more popular management literature. I think the book will be found useful by persons studying
for the Diploma in Management Studies, the professional examinations
of the Institute of Personnel Management, and university courses in
sociology, particularly since this is one of the few texts on organizational
change which concentrates primarily on British (rather than American)
source material.

Marlow   E. A. JOHNS

"Sociology seeks to explain the continuity of social systems through time. Yet continuity must be recognized at relative. . . . In any event, most of the societies which form part of the more recent history of man seem to have experienced an almost continuous, often pervasive, and sometimes highly accelerated process of change. Yet with change, as with continuity, the sociologist assumes that the sequence of events is orderly. The process of change is not random, even though it may at times seem chaotic, and is often beyond the conscious control of individuals and of society as a whole. Sociology, therefore, also describes change in social systems, and seeks to uncover the basic processes by which, under specified conditions, one state of the system leads to another, including, potentially, the state of disorganization and dissolution."

(Alex Inkeles, *What is Sociology?* Prentice-Hall, 1964, p. 27.)

Introduction

THE material in this book has been directly inspired by the belief that the manager of the future must be a "do-it-yourself behavioural scientist"*, capable of investigating and acting upon a whole range of problems of industrial relationships within his organization. Indeed, so relevant are Professor Lupton's views in this present context that it is worth while restating them briefly in order to justify the study of organizational change as an appropriate topic for the manager. Lupton starts with the basic and incontestable premise that all company decisions relating to the survival, profitability, and reputation of the company have behavioural implications, especially strategic choices governing the technological means to be employed, the scale of operations, the structuring of management, location and layout of plant, and methods of salary and wage administration.

The personnel manager could perform potentially an indispensable function of advising on the human and social consequences of projected changes as such, as well as the probable implications of implementing these changes in particular ways. Yet personnel management is not, at present, equipped to fulfil this new and future role adequately, and it is by no means certain that its existing functions and practices are even being modified in the desired direction†.

In 1964, Charles Myers wrote: "The central fact of industrial life in the second half of the twentieth century is the accelerating pace of basic scientific knowledge and its impact on technology. The revolution in information technology through the advent of the electronic computer

---

* These words were first used by Tom Lupton (*Industrial Behaviour and Personnel Management*, IPM, 1964, p. 22) to describe the developing role of the personnel manager, but since, in a very real sense, all managers are personnel managers, it seems reasonable to extend the argument beyond its original context.

† Apart from minor moves like the increasing emphasis on the behavioural sciences in the professional examinations of the Institute of Personnel Management.

1

is only one consequence . . . These rapid advances in our knowledge have, in turn, accelerated the pace of change, which today confronts management with new problems and has added new dimensions to old ones. Is the average personnel executive equipped to help management deal with these problems, or will he have to give way to the new specialists that are already coming to the fore—experts in information technology, in management of research and development, and in manpower and organization planning?"[1]

Three years later, Professor Dalton McFarland observed : "In organization design, manpower planning and development, and electronic data processing, line executives are already by-passing personnel departments. Meanwhile, personnel executives are not actively adopting objectives in these areas, nor are they trying to gain greater acceptance of the role of personnel in these areas from members of top management. Moreover, chief executives and operating executives do not seem surprised that the personnel departments are being bypassed."[2]

If this is so, personnel management will survive only as a relatively minor administrative aid to management, dealing with pensions, welfare, and the like, and restricted to "pulling human chestnuts out of the technological fire". This rag-bag view of the personnel profession must be uniformly depressing to the vast majority of its practitioners, not least because it implies a sterility and dyed-in-the-wool conservatism which could mean ultimately the disappearance of personnel management as a separate activity.

It seems to me far more stimulating and productive to take Lupton's argument that the personnel manager of the future will be a "social analyst", whose task it would be to forecast the range of social and psychological problems which would follow from a technical decision, and advise how the decision might be modified so as to minimize these —a preventive rather than a remedial job.[3]

Certainly the personnel manager must fulfil an important role in developing "social shock absorbers"[4] in companies facing technological change. This means, for example, formulating and announcing policies of not downgrading or laying off permanent and long-service workers, or coping with any inevitable redundancies in a manner least damaging to the organization or the individuals concerned. Such policies are clearly essential if change is to be accomplished successfully. Yet even if these policies originate within the personnel department, their implementation remains a responsibility of line management. Therefore, it is essential that line managers are aware of the behavioural implications of their own decisions without relying purely on the judgment of the personnel function. Apart from anything else, very few managers have their own behavioural scientists permanently "on tap" to offer advice whenever decisions with potentially dangerous repercussions are to be made.

For all these reasons, the line manager must appreciate for himself the complexities and difficulties of innovation and change.

Certainly the increasing pace and scope of technological and social change must eventually force organizations, which have hitherto been content to react to rather than to anticipate change, to consider more constructively the implications of such trends as skill obsolescence, retraining, future wage differentials, increasing social mobility and the restructuring of occupations (exemplified by the 'destatusing' of clerical tasks). In this context it is unfortunate, as Mann and Williams[5] have pointed out, that most studies of individual motivation, job satisfaction, organizational effectiveness, superior–subordinate relationships, work group characteristics, and so on, have been undertaken in organizations where relatively little change is taking place. The result is that companies undergoing reorganization or accommodation to some major technological change have rarely been examined. Possibly researchers are unwelcome at a time when the organization is already undergoing the period of stress which innovation involves. Although this generalization is rapidly losing much of its validity (largely through the achievements of writers like Crozier, Rice, and Burns), it is imperative to concentrate more of our energies and resources on the study of organizational change*. Such a shift in focus will not only increase our understanding of human behaviour in an organizational context, but will also supply us with valuable information about the most effective ways of managing change.

At present the danger is that the planning of technological innovation will be left entirely to technical staff, with the result that plans concen-

---

* As Warren Bennis puts it, "change is the biggest story in the world today, and we are not coping with it adequately". W. B. Bennis, *Organizational Development: Its Nature, Origins and Prospects*, Addison-Wesley, 1969.

trate on technical problems to the exclusion of all others, either human or organizational. A potentially disastrous situation of this kind can be averted by the appearance of a new breed of manager sufficiently familiar with the achievements of the behavioural sciences to be able to give, with reasonable certainty, the probable consequences of his own managerial decisions and strategies. Such knowledge could theoretically be gained by experience, through a long process of trial and error. Lupton, however, argues the need for "a more general skill, rigorously and systematically taught and applied, for the analysis of the problems of industrial and commercial organizations."[6] The essential characteristic of this skill is the ability to diagnose particular social situations, to interpret the findings of the behavioural sciences in relation to the problems of a particular organization, rather than to apply cut and dried principles.

The purpose of this book, therefore, is to collect much of what is known about organizational change and its implementation, so that managers can select those sources which appear to be of most relevance to their own situations. Where possible, arguments and generalizations are supported by research evidence rather than anecdotal sources, which are very often (although not always) of limited relevance. I have also used examples from my own research, consultancy, and teaching experience to give further depth to the material.

CHAPTER 1

The Need for Constant Change

THE ability to introduce change with minimum resistance is a key managerial skill, since change is a necessary way of life for all organizations. Even if a company intrinsically does not wish to change, it must eventually respond to movements in the social and economic environment if it is to survive. As Russell McFall, chairman of Western Union, has pointed out, the ability to manage a successful business now depends much more on outside forces. Yet "Companies fall into two classes : those who are standing and waiting for the revolution to come, and those who feel it's already here. In either case, they may find they have created a monument to technological feasibility which is really a business dinosaur. Like many other companies, we have gone from being a small single-product company to being a large, diversified multi-product multi-market corporation. Our customers are more demanding today. The numbers of decisions we have to make increases. The impact of each decision is growing. And we have less time in which to make them."[7]

Peter Drucker[8] has attempted to define the areas of change in society in the following terms :

(1) The explosion of the new technology which will result in new industries.
(2) The changes from an international to a world economy and the need for new institutions to meet these changes.
(3) The new pluralistic institutions which will pose political, philosophical and spiritual challenges.
(4) The new universe of knowledge based on mass education and its implications in work, leisure and leadership.

Rosemary Stewart's classification[9] is similar in content, even if the language is more sober and precise :

(1) Technological innovations, leading to new products and new methods of manufacture.
(2) Shifts in market patterns as a result of technological advance, changes in consumer wants, and new methods of selling.
(3) Greater competition, both nationally and internationally, influenced by tariff changes and currency restrictions.
(4) Changes in governmental regulations and taxation, hire purchase restrictions, and labour policies.
(5) New management tools, principally the computer.
(6) Changes in the background, training, and occupational expectations of employees.

The need for constant innovation in all organizations is thus inevitable. In commercial terms, new methods, new products, new markets and new techniques are the means of avoiding the stagnation which exists when profits are too low*. However, large organizations are more capable of withstanding the risks inherent in change than small firms. Large companies can afford market research, test marketing, advertising, and sales promotion. "If one product fails, the losses are carried by the profits on other products. They can experiment with new personnel policies, behavioural science, sophisticated methods of training. . . . They have little or no difficulty in borrowing money. The giants can even incur massive losses and yet survive, because no government can accept the consequences of complete closure."[10]

Small firms lack most of these advantages, but as we shall see, they have some merits of their own, such as the ability, unencumbered by bureaucratic rigidities, to respond rapidly to environmental fluctuations.

---

* Profits are too low when the return on capital employed falls below 15 per cent. At such levels, profits are an inadequate reward for the risk involved, given the obligations of corporation tax and dividends, and the requirement for some surplus funds to be ploughed back into the business. The average rate of return on capital employed in public companies is approximately 12 per cent, which means that many firms must be in a position where their owners would make more money by investing their capital elsewhere. Of course, there is no law against running a company for low profits, but it must be recognized that the assets thus committed could be better utilized.

Shifts in market patterns may arise because of developments within an existing market or because of increasing concern for new hitherto unexploited areas.

The European Economic Community, for example, represents a potential market five times as large as the United Kingdom. Many companies have found that the attempt to enter such markets is not merely a matter of selling a range of products already established, but requires fundamental rethinking of problems such as product design. The cutlery firm of Viners has had to adapt to the French practice of laying their forks face down on the table—to British eyes—so the pattern appears to be on the "back". Moreover, the composition of a place setting differs from country to country : seven pieces are common in Britain, four in Germany. Crittall–Hope, the leading British maker of metal (steel or aluminium) windows, must face the fact that on the Continent totally pre-fabricated windows are virtually unknown. Instead, manufacturers offer their own metal window and curtain wall *systems*, and sell extruded sections to small companies for making up to client specifications. Crittall–Hope could do the same, but to do so would entail a significant shift in the company's existing pattern of operations, since their present strength lies in manufacturing finished products in bulk. These two cases[11] illustrate the tentative and gradual way in which the process of change must be tackled in circumstances where the very feasibility of the change itself must be in doubt, and where planning for change must, of necessity, be flexible, capable of adaptation in the light of experience.

Changes in consumer wants can be illustrated by reference to developments in the market for frozen foods. The increased employment of females, especially married women, implies that the use of prepared foods is more acceptable, a fact to which the relevant companies have responded by producing frozen complete meals. Although it was estimated in 1972 that only five per cent of the British population owned home freezers, and only 60 per cent owned refrigerators, it could be reasonably assumed that these proportions would increase rapidly over the forthcoming decade. A consequent move towards bulk purchases of food requires a change in shopping habits from a weekly to a monthly accounting basis, but experience with ice-cream and pre-packaged meat (particularly poultry) has shown that this is feasible. Moreover,

increases in disposable income have helped to ensure that foods previously regarded as 'treats' are now purchased more frequently, and
the development of frozen-food technology means that housewives can
be more adventurous without committing themselves to an exaggerated
investment of time and effort in food preparation. In a remark which
should be framed on every manager's office wall, one of the senior
executives at Birds Eye said : "What we must remember is that the
present is totally inadequate for the future. Our philosophy is one of
perpetual dissatisfaction."[12]

Developments in the expectations of employees have always been a
particular source of concern for the personnel manager, involved with
such problems as the aging of the population and the influx of women
into the labour force*—two aspects of a basically unitary problem, the
difficulty of recruitment in a situation of acute scarcity. Yet personnel
policies, because they are, in a sense, two or three steps removed from
the direct effect of market forces, may be slower to react to environmental change than, say, the marketing and production functions.

For example, the experiences of Vauxhall Motors in 1966 illustrate
the dangers of continuing to operate personnel procedures designed for
(and therefore appropriate to) an earlier phase of the organization's life.
Undoubtedly one of the principal reasons for the sudden disturbances
in a previously outstandingly-peaceful company was the increase in the
size of the organization, both in numbers employed and in the spread
of its plants. To begin with, the labour force of Vauxhall Motors had
been almost entirely recruited from the Luton and Dunstable areas, a
locality formerly noted for straw hat manufacture, and the company
was relatively isolated from the vast Midland manufacturing areas.
Furthermore, Vauxhall Motors was small by comparison with other
motor firms. Today, Vauxhall Motors employs over 35 000 people, a
situation which has forced the company to recruit workers from a far

---

* The Equal Pay Act, 1970, with full implementation scheduled for 1975,
happens to be a stimulus for change which evokes resistance in a particularly
virulent and emotive form. As Edwin Singer says, "Many male employees will
find considerable difficulty in coming to terms with a situation in which women
may be promoted above them, have equal opportunities for training for the best
jobs, or can enter apprenticeships. Experience shows that men hang on grimly
to defend the bastions of what they consider to be male prerogatives." See
E. Singer, "Paying Women Equally", *Management Today*, May 1972, pp.
143–150.

greater catchment area and has shown, incidentally, that a management system of "benevolent paternalism" is simply not workable in a really large establishment. By 1966, increasing size had also attracted the attention of the unions and, in particular, the unofficial motor industry joint shop stewards committee. In virtually every respect the company's "splendid isolation" had been dissipated and yet, at that time, personnel policies had not been adjusted in recognition of this fact[13]. There have been several similar instances in recent years, where the basic provocation of industrial conflict has been the continued application of anachronistic personnel policies. This fact alone should point to the need for personnel departments to undertake continuous reviews to ensure that their procedures take account of the *current* situation in its technological, social, economic and environmental aspects, rather than reflecting the company's position in the near or distant past.

The risks which companies run by operating on the principle of letting change manage them rather than managing change for themselves are illustrated dramatically by the case history of Singer Manufacturing. At the time of its foundation in 1850 by Isaac Merritt Singer, the firm was far ahead of its time in its marketing, production and management techniques. By 1958, Singer was a conspicuous example of a company with a mismanaged heritage—"fat, complacent, ponderous, unimaginative and vulnerable"—with a miserable 2·5 per cent return on total assets. This situation was a result of the fact that once Singer had achieved its unique position in the sewing-machine business, its management simply congealed like cold porridge. In the words of Donald F. Kirchner, President of Singer since 1958, "Its very success led to the assumption that all the answers were found, and that all one had to do was do what one's predecessors had done before."[14] However, the sheer problem of survival (in the face of the import of sophisticated, low-cost sewing machines from abroad) eventually forced Singer to initiate revolutionary changes by rapid product innovation and diversification into non-sewing machine sales.

Another case concerns Lesney Products, manufacturers of Matchbox die-cast metal toys. From a humble beginning in 1953 with a model of the Coronation coach and team of eight horses, the company expanded rapidly. The share price multiplied nearly 100-fold between 1960 and 1968, while in the four years up to 1969 Lesney earned at least 60 per cent interest on capital employed. With profits on this scale, Lesney had to be prepared to meet competition, but they were totally unprepared for the form which this competition finally took when, in 1968, the American company, Mattel, introduced die-cast models with minimum friction wheels. Even when it became clear that Mattel's "Hotwheels" cars were establishing themselves, Lesney still adopted a wait-and-see strategy. As John Davis[15] has commented, "Had they not been a one-product firm, they would undoubtedly have reacted more quickly. But the very thing that made them so successful—the channelling of effort into one direction—was now working against them." Finally Lesney had to take action, if only because their existing range of products had virtually become obsolete. They needed new assembly lines, new machinery, new packaging, and a new image. The cost of getting them was at least £1 million and several nervous breakdowns. In this respect Lesney exemplifies another of the disadvantages of one-product companies. The more successful they were, the more commitments they accepted (principally expansion plans, to be financed out of anticipated cash flow) and the more difficult it was for them to unwind when something went wrong. Eventually they managed to recover, but in the process sought to ensure that at least 50 per cent of production and profits came from non-die-cast items, as an insurance policy against similar attacks in the future.

Perhaps the growing popularity of subjects like Business Policy and Corporate Strategy in the business schools and elsewhere suggests a more widespread appreciation of the necessity for anticipating change and taking steps to mitigate its impact, as distinct from simply following the "crisis management" doctrine of coping with problems as they arise. The contrast between these two approaches could not be better illustrated than by recalling the initial confusion within most firms provoked by the 1967 devaluation, compared with the well-planned and smoothly-functioning strategies prepared by Standard–Triumph.

In the field of technological innovation a similar distinction can be made between *entrepreneurial* businesses, which continually seek to be first in the market with some technical advance (Pilkington Brothers) and *managerial* businesses whose existence depends primarily on the purchase and subsequent improvement of technologies devised elsewhere (Metal Box).

International Telephone and Telegraph (ITT) exemplifies corporate planning and forecasting in its most advanced and sophisticated form. In Europe alone, where ITT has more than 300 subsidiaries (e.g. Standard Telephone and Cables in the United Kingdom), the annual planning cycle begins in the early spring with a visit to each subsidiary by planning specialists from ITT's European headquarters. As a result, each subsidiary formulates basic objectives for the forthcoming seven years. ITT-Europe co-ordinates and approves these objectives and over the following three months the subsidiaries draw up detailed plans, including budgets and sales forecasts. If any unresolved problems arise, these are dealt with at the annual Business Planning Sessions, held in September and conducted by the American management of ITT. To justify the company's belief that planning is the very act of management, senior executives are involved in planning every month of the year, for even if the six-month planning cycle itself is not in full swing, they must be preparing material for it or producing performance figures for the previous year with which to compare attainment against aspiration. In 1972, ITT had enjoyed 46 successive quarters of increased sales, dividends, and profits per share, but it is fair to say that the plans are principally geared to the avoidance of mistakes. They have helped to tailor the company not to fail, rather than to succeed, and to take risks only when the right return is guaranteed or, in other words, when it is not a risk. The management of ITT is aiming at steady organic growth rather than rapid expansion. Above all, this implies a control and safeguarding of the environment in which the company operates, a deliberate self-cushioning against disaster and chance. In a perceptive comment, Christopher Mansell[16] suggests that "It is for this reason that most managerial theory is the creation of the large-company psychology. The more a company has freedom of action, mobility and flexibility, the more likely it is to be small and not to need the theory. Conversely, as in the case of ITT, the managing of the large organization depends on the deliberate setting of parameters, of limits of action, so that within each of these limits, the greatest possible freedom to manage can be obtained."

The case of ITT also demonstrates another major development in business over the last few years, the growing international and even world-wide influence of the large predominantly-American organizations through the operation of subsidiaries in various countries. Professor H. V. Perlmutter has distinguished three stages in the process. In the first, *ethnocentric* phase, the managers are pioneering missionaries from the parent company, while in the second, *polycentric* period day-to-day control of the subsidiary is handed over to local talent. This, roughly, is the stage now reached by most European subsidiaries of American companies such as General Motors. Thirdly, comes the *geocentric* phase when the organization is genuinely international. At this point, managers are deployed anywhere in the world, regardless of nationality, wherever their talents will be most useful. No company has yet achieved this, although IBM, in Perlmutter's view, has come nearest to doing so. For an IBM computer, the central processor may come from Germany, the memory system from Japan, the tape from Sweden, the printer from Italy, and other ingredients from Britain*.

These trends are already having their effect in modifying cultural differences in management styles and behaviour, so much so that Galbraith and others have developed a "convergence thesis" predicting increasingly-similar national policies to ensure adequate purchasing power to absorb industrial products or a supply of trained manpower adequate for business requirements[17]. For example, while it is still possible to discern the special characteristics of the Japanese enterprise —poor communications, overwhelming stress on seniority, and the importance of life-long loyalty—these are changing under the pressure of "Americanization", for good or ill. The kind of management system typical of the U.S.S.R., described by Granick[18] and Richman[19], is also altering as Russia opens up its communication channels and begins to lose its pathological suspicion of all things Western.

On the other hand, the extent of the similarities between American

---

* Kaufmann adds Ford, ITT and Caterpillar among American companies; in Europe, the sample should include ICI, Nestlé, Ericson Telephon, Rhone–Poulenc, and Brown Boveri. Instead of employing Perlmutter's terminology, Kaufmann uses the phrase "multinational" to describe organizations where "strategic, administrative, and operational decisions are co-ordinated on a wide geographical scale." Organizations are "international", by contrast, if "their foreign operations consist of exports only, including supporting marketing activities." Examples include the Swiss watch industry and Volkswagen. See O. Kaufmann, "Strategies of Expansion and Organizational Developments in European and American Firms", *Journal of Management Studies*, Vol. 9 (1), February 1972, 82–96.

and Russian business systems has been greatly overstated, especially by Galbraith. As Child[20] points out, Galbraith equates far too readily the American mode of economic planning, decentralized at enterprise level, with the centrally-directed planning methods employed in Russia. Moreover, the validity of a longitudinal socio-economic hypothesis can only be established by reference to meaningful historical data, which are just not available, particularly for communist societies. At the level of the enterprise, it is clear that the goal of economic effectiveness, or mediating features like size and technology, are not deterministic constraints on organizational structures or managerial behaviour, while the culturally-induced expectations of those entering work must remain an additional factor making for differences in structural patterns and style.

In seeking to insure itself against the uncertainties of the future, a company may well seek to introduce new products in its own field or diversify into totally unrelated activities. Very few firms (Coca-Cola is a rare exception) can hope to achieve substantial growth by depending on one product alone. Some organizations learn the lesson of diversification the hard way, for example the Fairchild Camera and Instrument Corporation, Long Island. In January 1958, without any warning, the U.S. Air Force cancelled Fairchild's contract for B58 bomber reconnaissance cameras, which at that time provided the company with 85 per cent of sales. The firm's eventual recovery from this crisis and establishment of a commanding position in micro-miniaturized integrated circuits has been described as a first-class demonstration of "skilled technological management, gambling with maximum stakes from a minimal position"[21]. It is at least clear that Fairchild was sufficiently adaptable to learn from its mistakes, unlike many less fortunate companies.

Organizations with a properly-evaluated corporate strategy now see diversification as a matter of course, as a means of providing a broader base of risk so that any one technological trend has less impact on the company's overall performance. Thus electrical appliance firms such as General Electric and Thorn Electrical Industries have started to manufacture gas appliances (a protection against the possible impact of North Sea Gas), and American Telephone and Telegraph develops communication satellites in order to sustain its major role in long-distance communications. Diversification for other companies, although still a protective device, is seen principally as a means of faster growth and increased profitability. Examples in this category include Imperial Tobacco's excursions into the manufacture of crisps, frozen foods, and programmed learning, and W. R. Grace's transition into chemicals (which now provides two-thirds of its total sales) away from its original business as a shipping company with plantations and other interests throughout South America.

From the individual manager's point of view, the problems raised by diversification are much the same as the problems of coping with technological innovation, and lie basically in the manpower field. It is likely that the demand for particular kinds of labour is both rising and falling rapidly. There is a sudden demand for scarce specialists coupled with a tendency to hire people for jobs which, after a few years, no longer need to be done. In some cases, the existing work force may be unable to adapt to these fast-changing demands, and so the organization is faced with the task of retraining, replacement, or redundancies, each of which creates crucial and painful dilemmas both for the company and for the individuals directly involved.

The fact is that, despite the adaptive characteristics of man as a biological organism, resistance to change is an endemic feature of his work environment, and this is what makes the successful introduction of change one of the most difficult problems that the manager can encounter.

To be more precise, it is relatively easy to implement change in machines, materials and even animals, but much more difficult to cope with people because their responses are relatively unpredictable. "Lead them to water in an effort to make them drink and some, misunderstanding your message, may swim away. Others may give your message the 'file and forget' treatment. Those who are spurred to action may take a sip and then try to hold your head under. Those who comply obediently may respond with inertia or resistance on the next occasion. Some may be more interested in activating *you* than in being activated *by* you. . . . The selection of appropriate methods of activation is extremely difficult. Although activation is the use of power, or influence, this is not a mere matter of turning on a switch."[22]

Essentially similar arguments have been given elsewhere to show the impracticality of continuing to accept the egocentric notion that "organization change is heavily dependent on a master blueprint designed and executed in one fell swoop by an omniscient consultant or top manager."[23] Certainly if participative or pilot project methods are employed, detailed pre-planning is impossible, but even if this is not the case and precise procedures for the implementation of change are adopted, there are bound to be unplanned events as subordinates begin to "talk back" and raise issues that top management has not anticipated. Change, too, is one of those situations which raises the them/us conflict in its most virulent form (unless steps are deliberately taken to dampen down the issues involved). Many employees apparently lack any internal commitment to the change and are, therefore, extremely reluctant to take any initiative necessary for the change to be successful.

One further issue is raised by the fact that change takes time to plan and implement. If the change is directed at the solution of a specific and defined problem, it is quite likely that the problem itself has changed by the time the change process is complete. As Robert Heller[24] puts it, "if it takes two years to draw up a new shop-floor management structure in a car company, the problem won't be the same at the end as it was in the beginning."

A more detailed discussion of these problems and suggested techniques for resolving them follow in the remaining sections of this book.

SUMMARY

1. The ability to introduce change with minimum resistance is a key managerial skill.

2. Change is endemic in all organizations.

3. Resistance to change is endemic among people who work in organizations.

4. Large organizations can cope with unexpected change more easily than small organizations without going under, but the latter are generally able to respond more rapidly.

5.   Organizations must be aware of the dangers in continuing to apply anachronistic policies in the field of personnel (and other areas), if the organization itself and the external environment have changed since the policies were first formulated (e.g., Vauxhall Motors, Singer).

6.   Organizations can protect themselves against some of the "culture shock" effects of change by such devices as diversification, constant innovation, effective corporate planning, or the creation of international and multi-national systems that minimize the consequences of change in any one environment.

7.   Detailed pre-planning of a particular change is futile because, whether the organization likes it or not, people will "participate" in the implementation process; hence, plans for introducing change must themselves be flexible.

8.   Change takes time to implement and consolidate : by the time the process is complete, the problem which stimulated the change has itself altered—and so the need for change is never-ending.

CHAPTER 2

Change, Equilibrium and Homeostasis

AT THIS point it is necessary to make some *a priori* assumptions about the general nature of organizational change and its effects, in order to clarify the subsequent discussion on the desire of social organisms to sustain some kind of equilibrium and to seek to restore it if the existing balance is disturbed. It cannot be stated too emphatically, however, that generalizations in the behavioural sciences must be interpreted as probabilities or tendencies rather than dogma. It is, therefore, quite feasible that occasional exceptions to the rule will be found.

The whole organization is ultimately affected by change in any part of it. An excellent example of the radiating effects of change is the case of the paint room where women spray-painted wooden toys and hung them on hooks which carried them into the drying room. The girls were expected to reach engineered performance standards within six months, but the job was accompanied by serious problems of absenteeism and turnover. The girls claimed that the standards set were impossible to achieve (and in a sense they proved it by allowing many hooks to go empty into the oven). They complained of oven heat, fumes and in addition general messiness. The foreman decided to meet the girls and discuss their problems. As a result of their initial criticisms, directed primarily at the poor ventilation, the foreman obtained management approval to install three fans, which had a substantial impact on the girls' attitudes. At a second meeting the girls asked to be allowed to control the conveyor speed themselves, so that they could vary it during the day. After meetings between the foreman and the time study men, this idea was tried by inserting a Slow/Medium/Fast control on to the conveyor system, so regulated that "Medium" was a little faster than the previous standard speed. The girls experimented with their new-found freedom and eventually established the following pattern. For the first half-hour each day, the control was set at "Medium", while for the next $2\frac{1}{2}$ hours it operated at "Fast". For the half-hour before and after lunch the control was set at "Slow", and thereafter it operated at "Fast" until changed to "Medium" for the final 45 minutes of the day. The girls now reported that the pace was comfortable, scarcely a hook went empty into the oven, and rejects levelled off. Girls within their six-month learning period were collecting their basic pay, augmented by a learner's bonus and a regular bonus for production that varied between 30 and 50 per cent above the standard[25].

This story is often used to justify the potential merits of participative management and consultation, but it also demonstrates dramatically how success in implementing change in one part of the organization may be accompanied by disaster elsewhere. The girls in the paint room were earning more money than skilled workers in other parts of the plant, who exerted strong pressure on management to restore the status quo. Furthermore, the increased productivity in the paint room had not been matched in other sections of the factory, with the result that a vacuum occurred in the immediately preceding department, coupled with a bottleneck in the toy-packing section. Faced with these pressures, the shop superintendent revoked the learning bonus and restored the painting operation to its original methods so that the hooks again moved at a constant speed. Production dropped, and within a month all but two of the girls had left; after a few more months, the foreman departed. For the record, the abrupt cancellation of the experiment was not the only option available to the shop superintendent, since it is at least operationally feasible that a new equilibrium could have been created by applying the consultative methods, which had worked so well in the paint room, to all other sections of the plant, rather than simply seeking to restore the old equilibrium.

It is very hard to foresee all the major problems involved in organizational change. The unanticipated bottlenecks and vacuum effects experienced in the toy factory provide a relevant illustration of this particular phenomenon, but more significant examples can be found from the experience of mergers and acquisitions. The logic of such moves is based on the concept of synergy or the "$2 + 2 = 5$" process, where the combined resources of two companies in the same or similar businesses should or could achieve better consolidated performance than the individual firms could attain in isolation. It is true that some acquisitions fail because, in reality, the synergistic climate is not so favourable as first thought. Perhaps the details of the acquired company were not adequately investigated. But, as Simon Majaro[26] points out, "even where acquisitions are planned in what appears to be a perfect fashion, things often go wrong. . . . In most situations, the cause of failure is the fact that the organization is ill-equipped to cope with the strategy; that is, it is unable to absorb the new arrival, either completely or in part."

Thus a large British company making machinery for the glass, chemical, and paper industries adopted a conscious carefully-conceived strategy of growth through acquisition. Several companies in similar and complementary businesses were acquired in quick succession. Some were absorbed in their entirety while others were allowed to continue as semi-independent subsidiaries. Very soon, two problems emerged. First, the span of control of the chief executive was becoming un- manageable. Secondly, the acquired companies had been involved in a number of peripheral activities whose incorporation into the main- stream corporate objectives of the parent firm was difficult to achieve. If these peripheral activities were allowed to remain where they originally belonged—in the acquired companies—they might constrain the synergy sought by the acquisition. On the other hand, if they were allowed to remain semi-independent, they might absorb too much of the chief executive's time. The easy answer would be simply to sell the peripherals, but as Majaro comments, "divestment without proper business plans and opportunities appraisal is tantamount to throwing out the baby with the bath water." Given that the problem was organiz- ational in origin, perhaps the ultimate answer would be the appointment of a director with special responsibilities for corporate development, synergy and acquisition strategy*.

In a recent report[27] on his consultancy assignment with a large American corporation, Saul Gellerman has emphasized management's need to watch out for the unanticipated side-effects of change and the need for regular feed-back of shop-floor feeling. The company had suffered increasingly severe industrial relations problems for some years, culminating in a three-month strike at one of its largest plants. To

---

* It is interesting to note how, for psychological reasons, the term "merger" is used far more often than "acquisition" even if, in practice, the merger is an acquisition under the guise of a marriage between equals. Mergers enjoy greater social acceptability, to the community and to the affected employees alike, whereas acquisitions have obvious connotations of victory and defeat.

improve matters, management had introduced competition between the three shifts in the factory, rewarding those managers who did best. This move had the desired effect in that production rose, and management displayed improved morale. However, the company had failed to allow for the fact that there are two ways of winning a battle : one to do better yourself, the other to make the competition do a worse job. Employees had chosen the latter alternative. They failed to leave expensive tools in place for the next shift. They failed to pass on information to the next shift. They did the easiest work, leaving the more complicated jobs for the men who came in next. Even more important, the workers had formed the view that management was mad and irrational to let these practices continue. A large number of workers proudly quoted the published figure of the amount the company had lost during the strike, saying "That will show those bastards". In Gellerman's view the way the factory operated had reduced the men to a childlike role and they reacted by behaving like children*.

Technological change is a human relations problem as well as a technical problem. Mann and Hoffman have described the case of an electricity supply company erecting a new power plant, more highly automated than its existing installations, which throws some light on the importance of this proposition[28]. Although the new plant was geographically distant from the other (older) plants, and did not replace them, the workers in these older plants were directly affected. Their overtime was reduced as the company came to depend more on the lower-cost plant, and acute feelings of job insecurity developed. In a survey, 87 per cent of the employees at the old plants felt they would be made redundant if the company ever decided to reduce its workforce, compared with only 14 per cent of the workers at the new plant. Thus, from the point of view of the total organization, the high morale of the workers at the new plant was offset by the insecurity and low morale felt by workers at the old plants, a possibility which the company had never anticipated.

Response to change is conditioned by the individual's attitudes, which are in turn structured by his personality, his socio-economic background,

---

* Despite Gellerman's analysis, the company eventually decided to keep the competitive shift system because of the enlivening effect on the managers and on production.

and the work (especially the group) environment. One further reason for the complexity of analysing organizational change is that its impact is not a straightforward stimulus–response process. In fact, reactions of employees to change are determined by their own *perception* of the change, a fact revealed by the Hawthorne studies on the effects of lighting on productivity. Even when the degree of illumination was reduced, output continued to rise until the lighting reached 0·06 of a foot-candle, about equivalent to moonlight. "Not until this point was reached was there any appreciable decline in the output rate."[29] Understanding these situations is made even more difficult by the necessity for realizing that an individual's interpretation of change is often influenced strongly by considerations of group loyalty. This phenomenon helps to explain the apparent illogicality of large-scale strikes in which comparatively few people actually wish to withdraw their labour. Many of those who comply with the strike order may do so primarily because it seems to provide their only real opportunity for expressing dissatisfaction, or simply because it is a chance to re-establish the solidarity of the group by joining with it in concerted action*.

In contemplating the introduction of change, therefore, it is important to take account of the perceptual differences which are basically responsible for the varying reactions to, for example, the installation of a computer. Top management may see this innovation as an organizational triumph and a tremendous source of pride. The computer specialists see nothing but a series of delightful technical problems. Because, for them, computers mean attractive salaries and rapid promotion, they cannot understand that other groups may look at data processing systems from any other point of view. The lower-level employees (particularly the clerical staff), however, almost certainly see the computer in unpleasant and threatening terms. As Enid Mumford has suggested, they probably have friends who have experienced the traumas of computer introduction; they will have seen humorous cartoons depicting small lost clerks looking for colleagues in offices full of pulsating machines; worse still, they foresee redundancies.

Specifically, for example, a study by Mumford and Banks[30] found that bank branch managers felt their control was threatened by the

---

* In this sense the strike serves a somewhat similar function, in anthropological terms, as Christmas festivities, marriage feasts, and head-hunting rituals.

computer. A further study by Morenco[31] of the same process occurring in a French bank showed how these threats became reality; credit facilities were given to customers based on a "risk factor" supplied by the computer. Many managers felt they had been downgraded to "section heads", and that only the innovators and the computer services group felt any satisfaction from the change.

Individuals, groups and social systems are constantly seeking equilibrium, and management's general objective in implementing organizational change is to restore the social equilibrium and personal adjustment which change upsets. Common sense suggests (and research evidence proves) that people like to develop an established and familiar set of relationships with their environment. They learn acceptable ways of behaving towards each other, how to perform their jobs, how to accommodate themselves to group norms. They develop expectations about the actions of others which are reinforced by experience. When this state of personal equilibrium is reached, the individual no longer has to devote conscious effort to his own behaviour patterns because he has internalized satisfactory responses and modes of action. His position is comparable with that of the car driver whose long experience has left him with the ability to respond automatically to the various appropriate stimuli in the car and on the road. The driver can continue in this state of equilibrium so long as there are no significant changes in the environmental content of the equilibrium. But if, say, he moves from a car with a manual gear-change to another with automatic transmission, he must undergo a somewhat disturbing and uncomfortable period of unbalance or disequilibrium before he can achieve a new adjustment with his environment.

An identical sequence, progressing from one equilibrium through a phase of disorganization to the final restoration of equilibrium at a new level, comes into operation whenever social systems are subjected to change, except that the process is complicated by the dynamic construction of the human group. "Since every group is a social system, any change in one of its component parts is likely to require or result in alteration or rearrangement of other parts."[32] This network of individual and group relationships characterizing the social system is likely, indeed, to be so finely balanced that a final state of harmony is never attained—especially if, as seems highly probable, the achievement of equilibrium in one part of the system immediately precipitates disequilibrium elsewhere. Such a state of affairs will be familiar to readers of Mary Parker Follett. "When we think that we have solved a problem, well, by the very process of solving, new elements or forces come into the situation and you have a new problem on your hands to be solved."[33]

Nevertheless, despite the fact that social systems may be seeking the unattainable, they continue to strive towards social equilibrium by developing a series of self-correcting mechanisms which try to restore the balance whenever change occurs. These mechanisms are an application of the biological principle of *homeostasis*, the desire to establish a steady state of need fulfilment which implies the mobilization of protective resources if the "optimum" adjustment is threatened. "The reason why all big organizational systems work is to be found in Nature. We are not up to our necks in insects, although the little chaps breed fast enough to cover the terrestrial globe to a depth far exceeding our own height every summer, because there is an intricate interplay between the prey and the predator. Insect populations are 'under control' —not because of an authoritarian system, not because of an efficient bureaucratic machine, but because they are self-regulating. This property of homeostasis derives from a particular kind of structure by which the parts of the system are related."[34]

Viewed as a whole, the concept of *social equilibrium* involves a system of inter-related parts in a dynamic state of motion, whose essential attributes comprise *interdependence* (since change in one part of the system affects all the other parts) and a homeostatic tendency to maintain a steady state in the face of pressures for change. It is essential to recognize that the concept of equilibrium is not inconsistent with the presence of some friction and conflict, since the continuous interplay within a social system inhibits the attainment of an idyllic state of perfection. At the macro-sociological level, this view justifies the conception of society as a "tension management system" since "a society encompasses conflict and its associated change as well as a social order that comprises tension-preventing and tension-managing devices and systems"[35]. And, as Durkheim remarks, a society designed to eliminate conflict and tension soon becomes moribund. This fact, however, does not prevent some managements from deliberately manipulating their own social systems so that the existing equilibrium is not disturbed in any way. An example is the behaviour occasioned by the strong anti-union attitudes typical of U.S. textile managers. Few of the American Thread Company's plants are unionized and "Deliberate measures are taken to ensure that this situation does not change. For example, one mill which had 'the union' was given a wage rise in response to a union claim; the other mills were given a bigger increase. Then, six months later, as an act of apparent generosity, the bigger rise was given to the unionized mill as well. 'You should see what that did to the union', comments an executive of the company with evident satisfaction."[36]

Perhaps a situation which illustrates the phenomenon of a dynamic social equilibrium most satisfactorily is the moderate degree of upward mobility characteristic of advanced industrial societies. According to most of the available evidence, non-mobility can be seen as a mild form of deviance, the dying remnant of a dead-end equilibrium manifested in the so-called "rich full life" of the traditional working-class communities described by some sociologists. If this is so, and if downward mobility is viewed as being so culturally deviant that it can only occur under some initial predisposing handicap in physical or mental health, then it is quite feasible for upward movement to become the acceptable norm of behaviour*.

* It is fair to add that these statements merely outline a theoretically possible state of affairs, and are not meant to be accurate reflections of existing attitudes in British society. In fact there is plenty of evidence that social mobility in either direction or even non-mobility can, in certain circumstances, cause acute distress for the individuals who experience it. Studies of mental health throw some light on the personal tensions, social conflict, and dislocation provoked by social change or stability, despite the fact that the results are often inconsistent and refer to somewhat atypical examples. S. Lipset and R. Bendix (*Social Mobility in Industrial Society*, University of California Press, 1959) argue that "people who are upwardly mobile, but *not* those who are downwardly or geographically mobile, have higher rates of mental disorder than those who are stationary. This suggests that it is not the anomic situation associated with mobility that is responsible for the greater vulnerability, because one would expect downward mobility to be at least as threatening to psychic equilibrium as upward mobility. It is therefore probable that a particular type of ego structure which results from a characteristic family environment is both favourable for upward mobility and vulnerable to mental illness." This view has been challenged by other studies which appear to show that downwardly mobile groups show greatest mental distress, whereas upwardly mobile people exhibit even better levels of mental health than non-mobile groups. Possibly this is because upward mobility requires deliberate effort and therefore presupposes appropriate aspirations and efficient personal mobilization.

The literature of behavioural science research in management abounds with descriptions of workers seeking to establish and maintain an equilibrium relationship with their environment, often in extremely difficult circumstances. The Bank Wiring Room was a typical case where a group of men agreed among themselves to produce at a given rate each day, consistent with their view of a fair day's work, and applied sanctions for non-conformity against the shirker and the rate-buster. In this situation, somewhat surprisingly, the degree of conflict was minimal because management was prepared to accept the men's own norms as reasonable.

Recently reported was the instance of the tinsmith's department in a British aircraft factory where the shop steward examined each man's pay packet on Friday afternoon and relieved him of any bonus he had received in excess of five pounds (the money went into a shop steward's fund). Clearly this practice, which incidentally had operated successfully for over 20 years, ensured that bonus payments, and therefore total earnings, within the group were stabilized effectively, which was the object of the exercise in the first place. Tom Lupton has described the attempt by management in a manufacturing company to change the methods of wage payment among a group of assembly workers in a way which also involved changes in established methods of working. Management saw their innovations as a good way of dealing with current competitive problems and as an obvious move towards greater efficiency and lower costs. The operatives, not unnaturally, perceived the situation in a totally different way, as an unwarranted threat to the status quo. They therefore decided not to co-operate in implementing the changes for reasons which, when one came to investigate them, appeared perfectly reasonable. Over the years the men had devised a system of booking piecework time which, in the face of anomalous job prices and a fluctuating supply of jobbing work, enabled them to stabilize their earnings, and they simply refused to acquiesce in any disturbance to this balance. Lupton summarizes this as "A classic case of a small group adapting to its environment, but one in which the group's attempt to achieve and maintain equilibrium runs counter to organizational strategy."[37]

Cases like these (and there are many more which could be

quoted*) exemplify the argument that resistance to change is basically founded on a desire to prevent an existing equilibrium from being upset. This is not to say that social systems cannot cope with any innovations. When the change is minor and within the scope of the social system's established programmes for dealing with change, adjustment is fairly routine. Alterations in wage rates by themselves, for example, do not normally constitute a major threat to the work group's desire to stabilize earnings both within the group and within individuals. When the change is major or unusual, however, the system may resist in all sorts of ways : by aggression, regression, fixation, absenteeism, resignations, requests for transfer, and "the expression of a lot of pseudo-logical reasons why the change will not work"[38].

It now seems appropriate to apply the concepts of equilibrium and homeostasis to a practical situation†. If a group of workers is producing at 70 per cent of the efficiency that might be expected on purely technical grounds, the output obtained can be visualized as a balance between two opposing sets of forces. On the one hand, certain pressures are

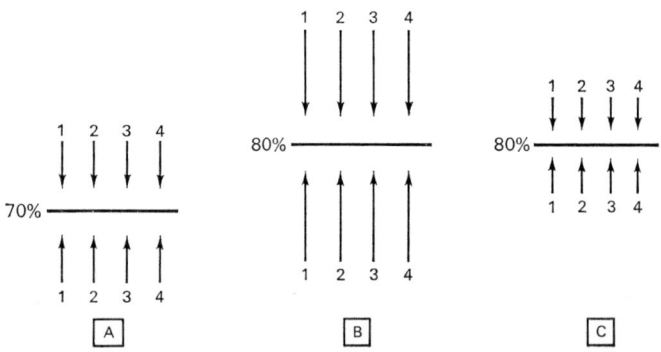

holding output down at the 70 per cent level, and for the sake of argument we may select four of the pressures which typically have this effect:

---

* However there are the occasional exceptions. Sheila Cunnison's *Wages and Work Allocation* (Tavistock, 1966), for example, portrays a highly-atypical degree of individualism among garment workers in a Salford factory. Equally, I have observed female operatives in a Devon engineering plant whose output norms—in the manufacture of typewriter keys—were peculiar to themselves and took no account of targets set by fellow workers.

† The following example is adapted from L. R. Sayles and G. Strauss, *Human Behaviour in Organizations*, Prentice-Hall, 1966, pp. 310–313.

(1) Dislike of the work itself.
(2) Fear of redundancy provoked by production at a level with which sales cannot keep pace.
(3) Informally set norms of output, designed to reconcile the desire for income with the discomfort of excessive or prolonged effort.
(4) Dislike of the supervisor.

On the other hand, if we view the situation correctly as a balance between opposing forces, there must be equivalent pressures holding output up *as high as* 70 per cent of the technically feasible maximum. Although seldom stressed by management for obvious reasons, these pressures might conceivably include :

(1) Fear of dismissal if output falls below a reasonably well-defined rate acceptable to or tolerated by management.
(2) Financial incentives like piecework, without which output would be even lower than it is at present.
(3) Fear of losing special privileges, such as concessionary prices for the company's products or the right to utilize company equipment for private work under certain circumstances.
(4) Pressures exerted by the supervisor.

Presumably, if these two sets of forces cancel each other out, the work-group is in a state of equilibrium, as represented in diagram (A). Management may be perfectly happy with this situation if it accepts a 70 per cent norm as reasonable. Alternatively, management may not like the situation but feel unable to do anything much about it because disturbances of the status quo are likely to lead to increased labour turnover which the organization can ill afford. In other words, the problem of replacing people effectively inhibits management action and appears to enforce acceptance of much lower standards of performance than in the past. However, if an attempt is made to improve productivity to, say, the 80 per cent level, management's typical approach is to strengthen the upward pressures in the balance of forces, a strategy known briefly as *overcoming resistance*. This it does by making the supervisor exert still more authority over the group, by creating more steeply graded piecework or incentive systems, by promoting fear of dismissal to an even greater degree, and so on.

These and similar measures generally have the desired effect (although they seldom raise output to the extent first anticipated by management), and production rises accordingly. But as the upward pressures are increased, so the downward pressures are themselves strengthened until a new equilibrium, admittedly at the 80 per cent level, is reached where the two sets of pressures are once more balanced. The crucial point about the equilibrium represented in diagram (B), however, is that stronger forces are operating on *both* sides. Therefore, tension and frustration are at a higher level and the workers are more likely to devise techniques for insulating themselves against the pressures acting on them. This is one of the reasons why Douglas McGregor argues that "A good individual incentive plan may bring about a moderate increase in productivity (perhaps 15 per cent) but it also may bring a considerable variety of protective behaviours—a deliberate restriction of output, hidden jigs and fixtures, hidden production, fudged records, grievances over rates and standards, etc. It generally creates attitudes which are the opposite of those desired."[183]

Overcoming resistance tends to be the basic strategy for change. As Lupton puts it, "Most significant organizational changes originate with higher management, and are 'pushed through' in one way or another. Resistance from the 'lower levels' is usually expected and plans are made to overcome it."[190] Overall, the approach appears to succeed because management works very hard, applies pressure, and knocks a few heads together (eliminating some, if necessary), but it does create resisting forces which are costly to organizational efficiency and flexibility in the long run, as well as damaging people at all levels. It is certainly one of the major reasons why organizational change takes so long to complete, if completion is taken to mean the end of the transitional period between one equilibrium and the next. Chris Argyris, commenting on 32 major changes in large organizations where he played some research and consultancy role, has said that not one was fully completed and integrated even three years after the change had been announced. "That is, after three years there were still many people fighting, ignoring, questioning, resisting, blaming the re-organization without feeling a strong obligation personally to correct the situation."[39]

One example concerns the recently published study of the methods used to put a productivity plan into operation at a large engineering factory[40]. (The plan covered a new wage payment system, a new wage structure and new machinery for consultation and negotiation.) As Gotting summarizes the position, "management sought to gain acceptance for their plan without subjecting it to an arduous process of bargaining with the manual workers. When opposition to the plan among the manual workers became apparent, management resorted to a strategy aimed at undermining their opposition." Having obtained the agreement of half the workforce to accept the plan, management attempted to win over the others by putting pressure on individual shop-floor workers. Not surprisingly, this approach provoked intense hostility from certain groups of operatives, culminating in a one-month strike costing the company £3 million in lost production. The eventual result of this direct confrontation was the factory-wide implementation of the plan. However, in the first six months after the full introduction of the plan 99 306 man hours were lost through strikes, meetings, walk-outs and lay-offs. In the following year 75 199 man hours were lost. During nine months of the next year (or between 18 and 27 months after the introduction of the plan) 216 588 man hours were lost through 45 separate stoppages. Clearly the plan had not attained one of its original objectives, namely, the "reconstruction" of worker-management relations.

Fortunately, management objectives can often be accomplished in a less damaging way by *reducing resistance*. According to this tactic, a higher level of production can be achieved by weakening the forces holding down output. The work may be made less disagreeable (through changing the technology or practising job enrichment). The workers may be induced to change their self-imposed norms, or to reduce their dislike of the foreman (even though this may involve replacing the foreman altogether). The result is likely to be the creation of the sort of equilibrium reflected in diagram (C) with greater output contrasted with a much lower level of tension and conflict.

In most real-life situations, companies tend to employ a combination of reducing-resistance and overcoming-resistance techniques. If we visualize these two strategies in terms of their capacities to create reward-oriented or punishment-oriented environments respectively, this approach appears to be soundly based on modern learning theory. Various studies have demonstrated the relative superiority of reward-oriented methods, whether applied to intellectual learning or behaviour therapy, and it will be sufficient here to mention two. In one experiment[41], 90 children aged between nine and eleven years were divided into three groups of low, average, and high ability. They were then further subdivided into groups to be given praise, blame or no incentive after performing a simple task which consisted of pressing the appropriate button (out of a choice of four) as quickly as possible after being shown one of four different words. When the task had been completed once, the announcement of the results to each group was accompanied by praise, disappointment, or no comment. The task was then repeated. On this occasion, those who had been praised performed at a much faster rate, while those who had been blamed acted more erratically and slowly. Thus, regardless of intellectual level (though the improvement was slightly more marked for the high-ability groups), praise had effectively raised performance while blame appeared to be an inhibiting factor.

In another study[42] of 42 people of average intelligence but with a variety of behaviour problems (mostly sexual) dating back about eight years in each case, three basic types of treatment were employed. One group was subjected to procedures emphasizing positive reinforcement alone, where the desirable response was elicited and then maintained by rewards of various kinds, such as social approval, praise, or tokens. A second group was treated by techniques solely dependent on negative reinforcement in which the undesirable response was eliminated through associating it with such unpleasant consequences as an electric shock, vomiting, or frighteningly loud noises. The third group received a combination of these two approaches : undesirable habits were punished but desirable responses were encouraged by thorough training and a system of rewards. In the analysis, it was found that the treatment combining rewards and punishment (given to the third group) led to a greater proportion of successes than either positive or negative reinforcement in isolation. Such a conclusion may appear self-evident and even platitudinous but nevertheless has far-reaching consequences for the inducement of behavioural changes in the industrial situation.

The most obvious ways to overcome resistance to change in the individual is to threaten him with punishment (dismissal or demotion) if he does not adjust, or to promise him some reward (generally monetary) if he does. Either of these techniques, taken by itself, carries serious disadvantages. The threatening approach may cause the individual to respond by leaving the organization altogether, by sabotaging the change once it has been introduced, or by implementing it in a half-hearted manner. In other words, the threat of punishment may be effective in telling people what *not* to do, but still leaves them a number of options for positive action which still militate against effective adjustment to change.

Equally, the promise of a reward is only effective if the individual sees the reward as something which he personally desires. If his resistance to change is largely founded on economic fears, then the promise of an economic reward is both relevant and likely to be effective. But economic rewards will be much less successful if non-economic criteria are responsible for his resistance. Should a manager be offered a salary increase when he moves to a new location, for example, the prospect of a higher salary may take a relatively low priority in his mind compared with his hostility to the new environment, his doubts about the type of work he will be required to undertake, and his fears about prospective colleagues. In effect, then, "The first step in building effective reward practices is for the company to make sure that the rewards it is providing are ones which are widely desired. This is a seemingly simple point that is often neglected. In day-to-day operations we frequently forget that, regardless of the value the giver or observer places on a reward, its motivational influence comes about only as a result of the value the *receiver* places on it. In effect, rewards that the company considers highly positive inducements may not be so regarded by many of the persons receiving them."[43]

It thus seems clear that satisfactory approaches to the problem of implementing change in organizations depend upon a thorough understanding of the causes of resistance to change in individuals. The next chapter will examine this topic in more detail.

SUMMARY

1. The whole organization is ultimately affected by change in any part of it.

2. It is very hard to foresee all the major problems involved in organizational change (but that is no excuse for not trying).

3. Technological change is a human relations problem as well as a technical problem.

4. Response to change is conditioned by the individual's attitudes, which in turn are a product of his personality, his socio-economic background, and the work environment.

5. Individuals, groups, and social systems seek equilibrium and will try to achieve a new equilibrium (using homeostatic mechanisms in the process) if the injection of change disturbs an existing balance.

6. Resistance to change is founded basically on a desire to prevent the existing equilibrium from being upset.

7. A strategy of "overcoming" resistance may achieve results, but at the cost of increased tension, frustration, and conflict.

8. "Reducing" resistance, a change strategy based on reward rather than punishment, offers more promise of success, but only if the rewards offered are those actively sought by the individuals concerned.

9. In practice, a strategy based on both reward and punishment is likely to be the most effective of all.

CHAPTER 3

Sources of Resistance to Change

INTRODUCTION

As we have seen already, individuals and social systems tend to resist change because they want to maintain an existing equilibrium. The inclination to oppose change is partially offset, however, by the desire for new experiences or a break from routine, and by the potential rewards associated with change. Some changes may even be welcomed (such as a salary increase), provided they have no negative connotations, like a geographical transfer or a hidden demotion—although the employee who is being demoted, and knows it, may accept the change quite readily if he realizes that he is being relieved of the pressures and tensions in his former position which he is no longer capable of sustaining. Yet curiously, most companies go to considerable lengths to conceal their demotions, using devices like salary increases, the creation of special positions (only possible in growing and complex structures), 'zig-zag mobility' combining demotions with subsequent opportunities for promotion, and what Goldner* calls the "trip to Europe" ploy. This latter is a procedure whereby managers sent for training outside the company include a proportion who need time to adjust to a career disappointment.

---

* F. H. Goldner, "Demotion in Industrial Management", *American Sociological Review*, Vol. 30, 1965, pp. 714–724. Goldner also describes the corporate division which used one of its geographical locations to "retire" men who could no longer meet its standards of expected performance. Unfortunately the division ran into trouble when the location became known as a dumping ground. "The effectiveness of that operation was essentially destroyed until the organization started to send men on the way up to the same location, mixing them in with those who had been demoted. . . . Thus, filling similar positions with both successes and failures creates an intermediary level and cushions the shock of demotion."

Other changes are so insignificant that resistance, if any, is barely noticeable, although incompetent handling of the change can build up resistance impressively by a kind of chain-reaction process. Furthermore, it is dangerous to categorize a particular change as trivial since it may be anything but trivial to the people directly concerned. The introduction of vending machines is a typical example. Management may stress the advantages of being able to obtain hot and cold drinks at any time of the day, without regard for scheduled breaks. From the workers' point of view this may be of no particular value, principally because it disrupts their previous opportunities for social interaction available at formally recognized times and probably in a location (the canteen) away from the immediate work environment. If the workers are performing routine and monotonous tasks, specified breaks serve the additional purpose of marking the passage of time in an otherwise featureless day.

All these considerations make it essential that an apparently unimportant innovation should still be handled with extreme care. In one case known to the author where a vending machine was introduced into a small company, enormous problems were caused by the fact that it was the managing director's wife who initially determined the appropriate "mix" for the tea in the machine.

The chain-reaction effect also seems to operate powerfully in circumstances where management assumes in advance that workers will resist a particular change and, therefore, releases no information until the last possible moment. This generally means that the impact of the innovation is magnified out of all proportion, with potentially disastrous results. In a large technical college some years ago, great efforts were made to conceal some changes in office layout from the office staff until the Friday afternoon immediately preceding the commencement of building operations. Somewhat naturally, the merits of the changes themselves were forgotten in the ensuing uproar over the authoritarian way in which management had behaved. The office supervisor resented the fact that even she had not been trusted sufficiently to be consulted about the changes; productivity dropped drastically; three of the ten typists left altogether, a situation which the college could ill afford in view of local recruitment difficulties.

All this upheaval could have been avoided if the organization had subscribed to Judson's belief that "A manager can achieve the maximum benefits from a change only if he is able to minimize resistance to it by those affected."[44] At the college, however, management continued to be convinced of the rightness of its actions, even after the event. Indeed, the intense reaction of the office staff when the change was finally announced only proved, in management's eyes, that a policy of secrecy had been fully justified in order to avoid equally hostile attitudes over a much longer period. In this way management's assumptions about the behaviour of employees turned out to be a self-fulfilling prophecy. By calculating in advance that the office staff would resist any change, management brought about a situation in which resistance to change was inevitable.

Another curiosity about attitudes to change is that work groups composed of intelligent people will not necessarily understand and accept change more readily than, say, groups of manual operatives. In fact, the exact opposite may be true. Perhaps this is one reason (although there are others) why professions such as solicitors, doctors and accountants tend to be highly conservative as a group. A recent study by Nicholas Georgiades[45] showed that teachers in secondary schools exhibit strongly reactionary attitudes (as compared with business managers) when confronted with innovation. This conservatism held good even when a statistical analysis was carried out to eliminate the bias of age. The principal lesson here is not that intelligence is positively correlated with conservatism, but that new methods and innovations generally have to be sold with exceptional care if groups with above-average intelligence are involved.

Resistance to change also has positive aspects. If resistance is simply a manifestation of the system's desire to maintain a steady state in which its survival functions can be performed adequately, it must play an important role in preserving the health of the system. "Nevertheless, resistance to change is frequently deplored without regard to its healthy attributes . . . reformers are apt to see resistance as 'wholly bad' and to project the badness on to individuals or groups, who then become both the reason for the difficulty and the excuse for inaction . . . 'Middle management' in industry and the 'old guard' of almost any institution are thus often condemned without reference to the essential service they render in maintaining their institutions."[46]

Change is not desirable as an end in itself, and opposition to change forces the advocates of change to examine their arguments more closely. Even if resistance is of an emotional rather than a rational nature, designed to protect vested interests rather than analyse the problem objectively, it still has several advantages :

(1)   It may help to identify pockets of low morale and motivation in the organization.
(2)   It can pinpoint communication weaknesses (on the assumption that resistance to change can arise from inadequate understanding of the reasons for the change).
(3)   It may force those initiating the change to give more attention to human relations on future occasions.

While not all changes are desirable, it is nonetheless true that those organizations which experience the greatest difficulty in introducing change successfully are those which only make infrequent changes. One possible (but controversial) answer to this would be to introduce change almost continuously—even if there were no compelling reasons. Some companies are virtually constrained to operate on this basis, partly because of the technologies which they employ and partly because of the presence of a relatively high proportion of "knowledge workers" whose expectations are geared to the introduction of change (so long as they are the change agents). An example is the American consultancy firm of Arthur D. Little, which has deliberately adopted an organic system that leaves little opportunity for reaching equilibrium at any point in time. The working pattern of relationships within the firm is frequently changing as case teams are broken up and reconstituted when old projects end and others begin. Each staff member normally belongs to several case teams at the same time and may even be the leader of one (because he possesses some relevant expertise rather than formal status). By reducing its dependence on a formal hierarchy, Arthur D. Little has avoided the possible dangers of simply replacing one obsolescent organization structure by another which would begin its own obsolescence before becoming fully operational.

It is true that a flexible structure hinders long-range planning, but the sole objective of such planning is to prepare the organization for future developments. This being so, the time-span over which planning should (and can) operate depends on the length of time needed to prepare for and implement strategic decisions. If the preparation time, or "reaction time", could be reduced, then the planning horizon can be shortened accordingly. This is precisely what Arthur D. Little has achieved. Its quick response to change is possible because the creation of new organizational relationships is less impeded by the need to break down existing relationships first. Employees are accustomed to change and welcome it; and substantial delegation of authority means that time does not have to be wasted in referring matters upwards for decision.

On the other hand, the impact of continuous change may merely be the creation of confusion, frustration, and low morale. Organizations are socio-technical systems, and any organizational change must take into account the social, as well as the technical, demands of the situation if it is to be successful. If management does want to pursue a policy of constant change, therefore (or if constant change is forced upon the firm by the very nature of its operations), it must do so against a background of security and stability which can provide a reference point for employees.

CHANGE AND THE SATISFACTION OF NEEDS

Resistance to change can only be understood completely if it is seen as a form of behaviour directed, as is all behaviour, towards the satisfaction of particular needs. Common sense suggests that these needs are organized in a systematic pattern; the most widely accepted arrangement is that developed by A. H. Maslow in 1943[47] :

(1) Basic physiological (survival) needs : hunger, thirst, shelter, warmth, and sex.
(2) Safety and security.
(3) Belongingness.
(4) Self-esteem and status.
(5) Self-actualization, self-realization and sense of achievement.

Maslow argues that these five levels are interdependent and overlapping, so that each higher level comes into prominence before the lower levels have been completely satisfied. On the other hand, if a particular need receives virtually no satisfaction at all, it is difficult for the individual to contemplate higher needs in the hierarchy.[48] Studies of workers in subsistence conditions suggest strongly that they give top priority to job security, earnings, and personal benefits, all of which are lower-order needs.[49]

For the most part, employees in Western societies have moved beyond the mere satisfaction of these lower-order needs, although Goode and Fowler[50] have described a Detroit automobile feeder plant where such needs predominated because of the lack of security and the ready availability of alternative labour. In one section of the plant, the work involved low skill and was done by physically-handicapped workers for whom the job was an economic necessity. In these circumstances, "produce or get out" was an effective sanction.

Even some fairly recent surveys of manual workers in the U.K. and the U.S.A. place a remarkably high emphasis on security, pay, and working conditions. Possibly this apparent paradox can be explained by class factors, the changing reference groups of manual workers, and cultural conservatism. However, the distinguishing feature of lower-order needs is that they are finite—the individual can reach saturation and even go beyond into a state of diminishing returns—whereas higher-order needs, from belongingness to self-actualization, are substantially infinite. For this reason, such motives are likely to be the dominant drives in advanced civilizations.

Belongingness needs are of special significance because they are exemplified in the post-Hawthorne vogue for human relations. McGregor argues[51] that while management may know of the existence of these needs, it makes deliberate attempts to frustrate them because it believes that groups represent a threat to the organization. Yet many studies have shown that "the tightly-knit cohesive work group may, under proper conditions, be far more effective than an equal number of separate individuals in achieving organizational goals." If the natural "groupiness" of human beings is frustrated, then people start to behave in negative ways, becoming "resistant, antagonistic, unco-operative."

Various studies of performance on assembly lines illustrate the importance of belongingness needs to workers whose lower-level demands have already been met. Walker and Guest[52] rated jobs according to "mass production characteristics" (noise, repetitiveness, restricted opportunities for social interaction) and discovered that employees holding such jobs often said that social isolation was an important reason for their dissatisfaction. The worker seemed to be oppressed by a "sense of anonymity . . . in spite of the fact that he declared himself well satisfied with his rate of pay and the security of the job."* If belongingness needs are catered for and then suddenly withdrawn, therefore, it is likely that productivity and morale will suffer. This has been demonstrated in a study[53] of workers in the voucher-check filing unit of an insurance company. They worked well together, kept up with the work load, and expressed feelings of satisfaction about their jobs. Their work area was inside a wire cage surrounded by filing cabinets and boxes through which supervisors could not see. In an alleged efficiency drive the cage was moved to a new area and the filing cabinets were positioned so that supervisors could see into the cage and, if desired, restrict worker interaction. The employees in the cage could no longer indulge in behaviour which was important to them (such as chatting, horseplay and eating), with the result that output declined drastically, the workers spent far more time on non-work activities, and their level of hostility towards management rose significantly.

A further important distinction between lower-order and higher-order needs in the Maslow hierarchy concerns the ways in which these needs are satisfied. Lower-order demands can be met adequately through the medium of money, whereas higher-order needs are generally satisfied through symbolic behaviour with a psychological and social content. Management may feel that they can avoid this problem by simply providing sufficient wages and then leaving workers to cater for their

---

* In a very few cases, some attempt has been made to offset the social implications of assembly line work. At the Philips plant at Eindhoven, a 104-man line was recently divided into five groups, with racks (bufferstocks) between each group. As a result, waiting time due to lack of material was reduced by 45 per cent, the workers earned more, they were glad to be able to get into the rhythm of the job, and absenteeism decreased. Bufferstocks had the additional merit of largely cancelling out the effects of system losses (time wasted through fluctuations in the individual's work rate). On a line of 104 places, without bufferstocks, system losses came to 16 per cent, whereas when the line was divided into five sections, they were reduced to $0 \cdot 2$ per cent. One of the major reasons for the improvement in morale once bufferstocks were introduced was the drastic reduction in group size. See H. G. Van Beek, *Occupational Psychology*, Vol. 38 (3 and 4), 1964.

higher-order needs elsewhere. This policy is unrealistic, if only on the grounds that the employee typically spends a third of his day (or half his waking hours) at work and would find some difficulty in satisfying *all* his higher-order requirements (especially belongingness) outside. Moreover, attitudes towards money tend to alter as the individual becomes more preoccupied with higher-order needs. Herzberg[54] has argued that salary is a "Hygiene" factor, coming into prominence if inadequate but seldom motivating the individual towards optimum effort. A study of incentive methods in the Belgian steel industry suggests that as more workers become "staff" (and consequently improve their status), so their view of straightforward economic incentives changes in favour of time-rate systems[55]. Managers, moreover, are seldom required to work within a direct financial incentive system, although they (unlike many manual workers) may reasonably expect promotion and this involves some financial incentive of its own.

Using Maslow's need-priority model as a reasonable interpretation of human behaviour*, it then becomes possible to classify, in relation to each need level, the particular anxieties which change evokes :

(1) *Basic physiological needs*
    Fear of reduced basic wages
    Fear of reduced bonuses
    Fear of demotion

---

* Most validity studies have confirmed Maslow's original assumptions apart from minor cultural variations mainly concerned with the relative ranking of the second, third, and fourth levels. A major cross-cultural survey of 3500 managers from 14 countries (M. Haire, E. E. Ghiselli, and L. W. Porter, "Cultural Patterns in the Role of the Manager", *Industrial Relations*, Vol. 2, 2, February 1963, 95–117) established that "The theoretical classification of the five types of needs according to their priority or prepotency exactly fits the pattern of results for the United States and England, but not for any other group of countries." Yet the discrepancies were not great. The study's most striking observation was "the relative similarity of thinking from country to country with regard to a particular need. That is, for example, those types of needs which are considered most important in one country tend also to be regarded as most important in other countries." More recently, it has been argued that "in a great number of situations, the three middle levels of the Maslow motivational hierarchy are not predominant, one over the other, and that the future would seem to hold a continuing increase of such situations." (R. A. Goodman, "On the Operationality of the Maslow Need Hierarchy", *British Journal of Industrial Relations*, Vol. 6 (1), March 1968, 51–57).

(2) *Safety and security*
Fear of technological unemployment
Fear of reduced working hours
Fear of the unknown
(3) *Belongingness*
Dislike of making new social adjustments
Fear of breaking valued social ties
(4) *Status and self-esteem*
Fear that the present level of skill in the job will be threatened
Resentment of the implied criticism that existing methods are inadequate
(5) *Self-actualization, self-realization and sense of achievement*
Fears that greater specialization may produce boredom, monotony, and a reduced sense of importance in the organization as a whole
Resentment over the inability to participate in planning and implementing the change

In view of the difficulty of drawing clear-cut distinctions between each of the five need-levels, some of these anxieties could well be classified under more than one heading. Because of their importance, too, some fears are worth discussing in more detail.

FEARS OF TECHNOLOGICAL INNOVATION

Undoubtedly one of the most powerful stimulants of resistance to change is the prospect of automation. Workers resist the introduction of mechanized equipment because they fear they will lose their jobs. Because they are understandably concerned about such short-run needs they are unimpressed by arguments about the provision of jobs in other parts of the country. Similarly, the craftsman may feel threatened by the likelihood that his skill will suffer a loss of psychological and social value*. Technological advances in steel plants, for example, require specialized knowledge in electronics and hydraulics beyond the range of the traditional electrician or fitter. The result has been the emergence

* For a detailed examination of this problem and its causes, see K. Hall and I. Miller, "Industrial Attitudes to Skills Dilution", *British Journal of Industrial Relations*, Vol. 9 (1), March 1971, 1–20.

of "supercraftsmen" or "technicians", implicitly entailing some erosion of status for the old-style craftsmen, a situation further accentuated by the elimination of the craftsman's mate.

On the other hand, raising the status of the job may be very helpful in gaining acceptance for change. Port employers in Rotterdam recognized long ago the need to upgrade port labour if technological innovations were to be introduced successfully. Today about 20 per cent of those employed in the docks are specialist winch drivers, crane operators, tellers, weighers. Rotterdam was the first port in the world to start dockworkers' training schools for boys of 12 and upwards, in four-year or six-year courses. These changes have increased the social prestige and status of port labour and have contributed to peaceful industrial relations in the area, especially when Rotterdam is compared with the situation prevailing in the London docks.

Unfortunately there is no really precise way of establishing what the employment effects of automation are likely to be. There are certain industries—such as oil, chemicals, and steel—which are highly automated wherever they are in operation, but Europe so far shows little sign of repeating the American experience where, over the last ten years, production has risen by more than 50 per cent and unemployment has doubled. The pessimists argue that the same thing could happen here —and that the unemployed will by no means be unskilled persons. They could include skilled toolmakers, comptometer operators, and even actuaries. By contrast, optimists suggest that automation generates as many jobs as it wipes out, or alternatively it is essentially no different from the process of mechanization which has been going on since the Industrial Revolution.

In 1960, the Royal Swedish Academy of Engineering Sciences concluded that the introduction of automatic devices has the effect of replacing skilled work with jobs which require very little training and know-how of the traditional type, while the demand for maintenance staff increases, generally by between 150 and 300 per cent. Galbraith, too, feels that "the industrial system reduces relatively, and it seems probable, absolutely, its requirement for blue-collared workers, both skilled and unskilled." He also observes, significantly, that management is not hostile to such developments because "a large blue-collar labour force, especially if subject to the external authority of a union, intro-

duces a major element of uncertainty and danger. In contrast mechanization adds to certainty. Machines do not go on strike." While it may
be true that automated organizations need more white-collar workers,
they "with rare exceptions do not join unions; they tend to identify
themselves with the goals of the technostructure with which they are
fused."[56]

In some cases the impact of technological change on the deployment
of skills can be modified powerfully by the actions of those principally
affected. As Miller and Rice[57] have pointed out, members of social
systems tend to become strongly attached to the existing order of things,
with the result that technical change is inhibited. In the printing
industry, according to Sadler[58], developments such as the introduction
of precision equipment in the composing room coupled with Linotype
and "Monotype" machines have significantly reduced the skill requirements among compositors. "Despite this, the compositor retains his
special position in the status system of the industry . . . Thus, radical
technological change in this industry has had rather different results
from those which might well have been predicted on the basis of any
study concerned solely with the way in which technology affects the
skill contents of tasks." Sadler adduces three main reasons for this
discrepancy :

(1) *The marginal position of composing work in a kind of "no man's
land" between "blue collar" and "white collar" work.*

The image of the compositor as "an artisan of superior intellectual
attainment" continues to be accepted, despite the fact that, empirically,
he can no longer claim this status.

(2) *The bargaining strength of the Typographical Association.*

The power of the printing unions stems from the fact that the product
(especially newspapers and periodicals) is highly perishable, and so
management is very vulnerable to the threat of a strike.

(3) *The strength and character of workshop organization in the
industry.*

The printing Chapels have a very influential tradition of solidarity,
equality, and democratic practice. According to Cannon[59], "Within the
Chapel, any status differentials which result from differences of work
or responsibility are reduced and all members are equal." "It is the
natural response of such a group," concludes Sadler, "to de-emphasize

the effects of change on the skills required for different jobs and to concentrate instead on the preservation of the social system."

If technological innovation is thought to imply redundancy, then the employee will resist even more strenuously. The experience of redundancy is traumatic, and characteristically people undergo four stages of reaction before reaching a new equilibrium[60]. The first phase is an immediate shock response which varies with people's positions and personalities. This is followed by a reaction known as "fight or flight", typified by the person who will not accept the situation and tries for arbitration, or by the person who simply pretends that it has not happened*. After this come the third and fourth stages of gradual acceptance and adaptation. Theoretically, this latter is the more realistic attitude which enlightened employers seek to develop in their departing employees, but to succeed in doing so requires that substantial warning of the redundancy be given beforehand so that the adjustment process is virtually over by the time the employee actually goes. It is perhaps instructive to contrast the uproar which followed the two-day notice of redundancy given to thousands of workers by the British Motor Corporation in 1956, with the orderly implementation of massive redundancies in British Rail workshops, whose employees were given between one and three years' preparation[61].

CHANGE AND CONFLICT

The process of change may itself generate resistance because it implies a substantial increase in the flow of orders to subordinates. Issuing orders has a powerful effect on interpersonal relationships in the sense that some subordinates resent taking orders at all. Others have become accustomed to a certain measure of control from higher management but strenuously resist any supposed attempt to increase management's ascendancy†. The sharp increase in control which accom-

---

* Fantasies are likely at this stage: the National Institute of Industrial Psychology refers to these as the "opening a country pub" syndrome.

† See the description of "punishment-centred bureaucracy" in A. W. Gouldner, *Patterns of Industrial Bureaucracy*, Routledge and Kegan Paul, 1955. The status quo is regarded as sacrosanct and any attempt by either management or workers to innovate or change procedures is fought by the other side because it is seen as a violation of the balance of power.

panies change undoubtedly threatens any feelings of autonomy and independence which employees enjoy. In short, it achieves the uncomfortable (and doubtless unintended) objective of emphasizing the subordinate status of subordinates.

A further problem here is that bosses and subordinates do not share the same perception of their relationships. In a study of the leadership styles used by 260 senior executives in 15 large American companies, Frank Heller[62] found that subordinates consistently over-estimated the extent to which they influenced decisions. Seniors also disagreed with their subordinates about the amount of skill involved in their respective jobs. Seniors thought that their jobs called for more of every type of skills except "technical skill" whereas subordinates believed that greater skill was required at *their* level in the case of seven out of twelve specific skills. None of these observations is particularly original or surprising, but they do emphasize that if subordinates are apt to perceive their bosses as autocratic in normal times, they are even more likely to do so during a period of change.

Initiating change by issuing orders is, in any event, a dangerous ploy. When told they must change, people often become stubborn and defensive, particularly if (because of the pressures on managerial time and the stress of change as such) the orders themselves are not accompanied by adequate explanations. Under pressure, managers have less time to devote to people. Even managers who are normally readily accessible to their subordinates tend to become remote, creating a communication breakdown which compounds the resentment already felt towards the change. Apart from these social pressures, change also produces physical strains in the sense that employees are asked to work at a more rapid pace and in a more devoted manner than normal. If overtime is required, even among white-collar workers, the level of conflict and tension during the change is raised still further.

If the organization is structured on staff/line principles, heightened conflict is a virtual certainty. Staff employees have a strong incentive to promote change because it increases their prestige and helps to justify their existence—yet for precisely similar reasons, line people have a strong tendency to oppose change. Pettigrew, for example, draws attention to the dilemma experienced by the Operations Research specialist "by the interpersonal conflicts which arise from his attempts to introduce change on an often unwilling management."[63] As a result the O.R. man experiences a measure of role strain* because of this conflict between the aspirations he has for his role and the obligations he sees as expected of him by the organization. Mumford and Ward[64] suggest three possible ways in which these conflicts could be contained. First, the innovating specialist requires a clear definition of his role and functions within the firm. Secondly, he needs training in interpersonal skills, and thirdly, management must recognize that his innovating role is a difficult one. In Pettigrew's words, " 'change-agents' should be taught social skills and given a greater awareness of their own role and the implications for others of their activities".

DISLIKE OF RE-LEARNING

Change almost always imposes a learning burden on the individual. This makes life difficult because people generally resent the expenditure of energy on learning new procedures when (to them) their existing methods are perfectly adequate. The worker may prefer a routine highly-regulated job with a short job cycle which no longer requires conscious attention. Once a person has internalized work operations so completely that he is able to perform the job in a "preconscious condition", he "is unlikely to be favourably disposed to changes which return his work tasks to the point where he must again consciously think about them."[65]

It may be true that the number of workers who are content to perform their duties in a "preconscious condition", which Pym compares with the state reached by participants in some modern and primitive ritualistic dances, is not a significant proportion of the total. It is certainly clear, as Argyris has pointed out, that any satisfactions so derived can have little to do with positive mental health. Moreover, the important question is whether these observed attitudes "be established as a norm for future action or seen as a tragic sign of failed aspirations."[66] Daniel, in a critique on *The Affluent Worker* series[67], argues that "focusing on orientation to work as revealed by job choice decisions is

---

* Role strain is "felt difficulty in fulfilling role obligations." (W. J. Goode, "A Theory of Role Strain", *American Sociological Review*, Vol. 25, August 1960, 483.)

inherently conservative is so far as it directs attention away from changes that could be made in the work situation and focuses it on managing the 'fit' between orientations and existing tasks and roles."[68]

The impact of automation generally means a further simplification of work procedures which most operatives dislike intensely* and the creation of characteristic types of work centred around the monitoring of dials and gauges. Essentially, such trends imply the replacement of physical stress by mental stress, a transition which creates problems of its own, principally in terms of mental health.

S. Moos[69] has suggested that an additional way of reducing occupational stress would be to reorganize the division of labour so that workers can be transferred between jobs according to a regular routine. This would ensure that they are not permanently engaged on machine-minding, dial-watching tasks. It seems likely that the success of this gambit would depend largely on the nature of the alternative jobs being offered. As Herzberg[70] has pointed out, the worker's affection for or interest in his job will scarcely improve if he is simply rotated from one meaningless job to another, perhaps being allocated to tasks as debilitating in their different ways as the process of machine-minding.

---

* In the General Motors plant at Lordstown, Ohio, each person on the assembly line has approximately 35 seconds to perform his assigned task. Because of the time pressures, workers tend to miss an occasional car altogether or perform only part of their job, perhaps by putting in nine bolts when they are supposed to insert ten. The alienation experienced by many of the employees, relatively new to the motor industry, has been explicitly demonstrated by sabotage: "slashing of seat covers, caving-in of radios, scratching of instruments in the instrument panel, scratching of paint, tearing glove box doors, destroying or bending the shift levers." Ironically, the move towards increased automation was provoked by poor profit figures—a decline from $2126m in 1965 to $1976m in 1971—made more significant by the effects of inflation. In the short term, however, the goal of profit maximization is incompatible with the creation of a more individualistic system incorporating more satisfying jobs. Yet in the long run such a change may be essential if General Motors genuinely wishes to regain its former financial record. See A. Thomas, "Sabotage at Lordstown—How General Motors' Bright Star was Dimmed", *The Times*, 16 March, 1972. Perhaps the following remark by Lewis Mumford is relevant in this context. "Work in all its aspects has played a decisive, formative part in the enlargement of man's mind and the enrichment of his culture . . . what merit is there in an over-developed technology which isolates the whole man from the work process, reducing him to a cunning hand, a load-bearing back, or a magnifying eye, and then excluding him altogether from the process . . .? (L. Mumford, *The Pentagon of Power*, Harcourt, Brace, Jovanovich, 1970.)

Effective job enlargement (Herzberg prefers the term "job enrichment") involves some vertical rather than merely horizontal additions, such as :

(1) Giving the worker a complete natural unit of work.
(2) Increasing the individual's own accountability for his work.
(3) Introducing more and more difficult tasks not previously handled.

Feelings of boredom and monotony, although not peculiar to the automated factory, are likely to increase at operative levels precisely because it is the simple repetitive uninteresting tasks which are most susceptible to mechanization. It is said that in Coca-Cola bottling plants, the old method of inspection was to put four bottles of the finished product in front of a strong light so that the inspector could look for any foreign matter in the drink. This was subsequently replaced by a continuous conveyor system, but the job became so boring that every now and then a bottle of 7-Up is run through to see if the inspector is alert. The experience of General Electric in the U.S.A. has been similar in seeking employee co-operation in computer installations. "We have found that we sometimes must deliberately build human decision back into the system, even though it would be possible to run without it. We must do this in order to gain acceptance for the system."

Several studies have pointed to the value of such changes for economic as well as human reasons, and it will be sufficient here to quote one. Conant and Kilbridge[71] have described the change-over from assembly lines to single-operator bench stations in a mid-Western laundry-equipment factory as an example of a move made to reduce costs and improve quality. In both respects the changes justified themselves. Typically, assembly of a washing-machine pump had taken 1·77 minutes done by six line men, but 1·49 minutes when made by one man at a bench. Time losses were either eliminated or greatly reduced in many directions because imbalances in division of work on the assembly line were removed, and time taken to handle products and tools was minimized. Quality improvements were due partly to the responsibility which each man had for his own work (stamping it with an identifying mark) and rejects declined from 2·9 per cent (on the assembly line) to 1·4 per cent (on the bench work). Virtually every other index of performance and morale, such as absenteeism, turnover and sickness rates, showed an improvement.

A recent survey among 32 applicants of motivation theory in four European countries[72], however, discovered that job enrichment or work structuring does not evoke immediate feelings of enthusiasm. "If you begin talking about rearranging work, people will become anxious about their job security, or their ability to do the new work or to take on the newly-delegated responsibilities." First-line supervisors are especially resistant to the change, which they may well interpret as the virtually total delegation of responsibility to subordinates, while they themselves receive little or nothing to fill the gap created in their own jobs. Their fears may well be increased by the circulation of case studies about the success of experiments with unsupervised work-groups allowed complete freedom to determine their own internal working methods and organizational relationships*. Unless a conscious effort is made to alleviate the natural fears of supervisory staff, "antagonism will be created among a group whose commitment is most vital to the success of the new venture" in Wilkinson's words.

According to Nancy Seear[73], one of the most significant sociological changes brought about by automation is that "Workers are no longer organized in sections and groups, but tend to work singly or in very small numbers scattered throughout the factory, according to the layout of the plant." Geographical diffusion in turn has important effects on the relationships between workers, and between workers and management, by blurring the traditionally sharp distinction betwen manual and non-manual workers, and by reducing the average size of the work group. Since fewer employees work in the organization, the importance of labour costs is diminished and it becomes much more vital to keep expensive machinery working. Under these circumstances the level of

---

* Specific examples include Non-Linear Systems in California and Procter and Gamble's plant in Lima, Ohio. The former was discussed by A. H. Kuriloff, *Reality in Management*, McGraw-Hill, 1966. Speaking on the relevance of this experience to the U.K., Professor Thomason (at a seminar on participation organized by the Institute of Personnel Management in May 1970) has shown how participation in decision-making provokes a kind of backlash at middle-management and supervisory levels. "In some organizations this may mean the elimination of some grades, usually supervisory level, and the amalgamation of others." See *IPM Digest*, No. 62, July 1970.

wages is of relatively little significance to the success of the enterprise, but the pressures towards shift-work (which often entails the payment of monetary premiums anyway) become almost overwhelming.

On the credit side, automation seems to improve working conditions in several ways. It nearly always leads to a drastic reduction in accident rates. Ford in England claims that where automatic equipment was introduced, the number of cases of hernia fell by 85 per cent. Hernia, eye troubles, and foot accidents have virtually disappeared in the Ford engine plant at Cleveland, Ohio. Tinplate workers, in a notoriously accident-prone occupation, experience relatively few accidents in the highly-automated plants of the British Steel Corporation in Wales. Dangers to health have also been reduced in industries where employees previously had to endure a relatively high degree of exposure to toxic materials, such as chemicals and petroleum refining or in the pottery industry where silica dust has long been a hazard.

FEAR OF THE UNKNOWN

Another factor which deserves special consideration in any discussion on resistance to change is the individual's fear of the unknown. Newness is always strange and threatening, surrounded by uncertainties, even if it is superficially an improvement over the existing situation, like the prospect of promotion. How hard will the new job be? How long will it take to learn? What will it lead to, if anything? Will I be able to do it? Will I like my colleagues? Clearly one cause of fears of this kind is the lack of factual information accompanying many changes, and the obvious answer for management is to provide the necessary background data to remove as much anxiety as possible. Three points arise here to complicate this apparently straightforward and even naïve advice.

Firstly, the mere provision of factual information will not remove all the uncertainties associated with change. No one can dispel entirely the anxieties created by the individual's own fears of how *he himself* will react to the new situation, no matter how many "facts" he has at his disposal. Just as a hospital patient about to undergo a particular operation is not altogether reassured by the knowledge that many others have survived it successfully, so a manager receiving promotion or an operative facing the prospect of familiarizing himself with a new machine both feel tense and anxious about their own possible reactions. In short, effective communications can only reduce fears but cannot eliminate them altogether.

Secondly, if management is to provide factual data in an attempt to overcome the anxieties provoked by change, it must know the precise source of these anxieties and it must offer equally precise reassurances, with quantified facts and figures, if resistance is to be appreciably modified.

Cases of geographical transfer on a company-wide basis show the kind of effort which is needed. In a recent example involving a total change from North London to a new town 30 miles away, the company arranged a series of free coach tours for its employees and their families which did much to dispel fears about the alleged remoteness of the new town, the cost of living there, the educational facilities, and so on. Senior company personnel outlined what the organization was trying to do and why, and what steps they were taking to consider their employees' welfare, while representatives of the new town's Development Corporation took parties round to see the shops, schools, locations for new houses, and typical show houses. This case, incidentally, also demonstrates the knife-edge dilemma experienced by people facing such changes. If they moved to the new town they would have to cope with new working conditions, different supervisors, colleagues or duties, and would have to fit into a new social environment; alternatively, if they remained in North London and became redundant, they would have to obtain a new job among entirely different work associates (whereas they would at least know some people if they stayed with the firm), with the additional dubious prospects of retraining, reduced earnings, and increased insecurity. In the face of so many imponderables, a single apparently insignificant factor could swing the balance towards an eventual decision, and this too is why it is vital for management not to avoid or omit even the most trivial points from its own communications programme.

Thirdly, factual information can only be effective if management anticipates the questions which will be asked by employees when change is imminent and publicizes the answers before rumour has a chance to gain a foothold. The danger here is that the company, in its anxiety to scotch rumours (if, say, a reduction in overtime has led to fears that the factory will be closed), may close options subsequently needed or, by going back on its word at a later date, may establish a credibility gap that takes a generation to remove. Experience suggests that it is very difficult to plan changes in detail. The normal processes of redeployment and reorganization are likely to lead to various alterations in the plans, to reversals of previous decisions, to experimental lines of action which later have to be modified. While such empiricism is justified by the circumstances, it is liable to be interpreted by workers as evidence of management's duplicity.

Management may be justified, then, in saying as little as possible about the proposed change until all the details have been settled in their entirety. By this time, however, rumours exaggerating the potential threats of the change would be widespread, with disastrous implications for the success of the change as such. People accept change, generally speaking, much more readily if they understand the reasons for it and if they are given ample warning so they have time to become accustomed to the idea well before being personally affected.

The importance of good communications, particularly in a period of change, is illustrated in the following case* of a Midlands engineering company which, up to 1958, had specialized in making metal fittings for the furniture and building trades. It then decided to diversify, a move which entailed the installation of a major extension to the factory and an increase in employees from 120 to 190. "Although there was no reason for concealment, the company never announced its extension plans. When staff asked questions about the new building they could see going up they were told that a statement would be made in due course. The works manager intended to give an outline of the plans to a Works Council meeting about a month before the new extension opened, but on the day of the meeting he was called away to a conference with one of the new customers. No statement was made about the expansion, but a notice was displayed giving brief details and stating that some staff, who would be notified later, would be transferred to the new production lines. Eight days before the start-up date notices were posted listing some 30 people to be transferred. Some of them objected, but in all but two cases the objections were overruled." The changes

---

* Adapted from Frank Broadway, *The Management Problems of Expansion*, Business Publications, 1966, pp. 128–129.

necessitated an increase in the number of lunch-time sittings in the canteen from two to three, and it seemed that the last (and unpopular) sitting had been allocated exclusively to people in the "old" part of the factory.

On the day of the change and immediately afterwards, there was a virtual boycott of the canteen, and production was extremely low on both the new *and the old* lines. Even when the inevitable technical bugs had been ironed out, output rose very slowly and only reached target levels after two months; meantime, management was having desperate trouble in meeting its sales commitments and some new customers were threatening to cancel their contracts. The unanimous conclusion eventually reached by management was that "people were not trying quite as hard as they usually did". However, when the firm expanded again in 1962–1963, it employed a totally different approach, using the lessons learned from its previous experiences. "The expansion was announced to the staff and to the local newspapers as soon as it was decided on. Ten weeks before the new extension was due to open employees were invited to apply for transfer to it. The response was good, and the people selected were told individually a month before the transfers became effective. The Works Council was invited to discuss the canteen arrangements following on the further increase in staff, and its recommendation was put into effect. Within one week production was on target in all sections, and a few days later the new plant was producing 10 per cent above its target level."

AGE AND SENIORITY

Closely associated with fear of the unknown in determining resistance to change is the factor of age, since anxieties about the future understandably begin to accelerate significantly with advancing years. The comparative hostility to change of the older worker has been studied principally in the context of geographical and occupational mobility, but many of the results obtained are equally applicable to technical innovation. A small but not untypical example is quoted in Garfield Clack's study of a British car factory[74] : "A new bin identification system was introduced in the spare parts stores and was, on balance, superior to the old method. The new system was fully adopted only after transfer (for other reasons) had removed the older workers from that section." Apparently trivial incidents of this kind give rise to the widespread assumption, dangerous and occasionally disproved, that older workers are either unwilling or unable to adapt to technological change.

Two principal types of technological change, characteristic of current trends, are responsible for aggravating the problems of the older worker. On the one hand we can see a gradual elimination of the so-called sensory-motor skills (that is, those skills requiring co-ordination of hand and eye), and on the other, an increasing demand for people to watch dials and gauges, making little or no productive contribution but being on hand to detect signs of malfunctioning should they occur. Unfortunately people in general are not very well adapted to dial-watching tasks and research into changes in capabilities which occur with advancing years suggests that the older man cannot compete so well in tasks with high demands on sensory acuity, large information throughputs, and (most important of all) tasks which involve swift paced work. The irony of the situation is that as the population becomes older (half the men employed in Britain are over 40), the climate of change favours the task, common in mass production and process production, more suited to the younger man.

Various studies confirm[75] what common sense would lead us to expect, namely that occupational mobility is inversely correlated with age. What are the reasons for this relationship? The older worker undoubtedly has many specific fears—such as the prospect of retraining with its problematical results and the extra fatigue associated with acquiring new habits—but seniority and security are often uppermost in his mind. Michel Crozier[76] found that neither job, nor age, nor factory made a significant difference in determining attitudes towards mechanization in a large French manufacturing concern, but seniority was decisive. This suggests that opposition to mechanization is a learned attitude : "workers become hostile little by little through a sort of learning process corresponding to their acculturation in the workers' group. The important factor seems to be the norms of the group and not the peculiarities of the situation."[77] The significance of seniority is also emphasized by the activities of trade unions, so much so that the relationship between job seniority and mobility is even clearer than the relationship between age and mobility*. In the steel industry, for example, there is a clear hierarchy of skills up to higher crew levels and the individual must inexorably move up one step of the ladder at a time as he passes through the long "apprenticeship" of experience. Steep earnings differentials between each step are acceptable even to the low-paid because with the passage of time they inevitably move towards the top of the ladder. Not surprisingly, labour turnover is low, for departure from the industry (with all the risks which that involves) would mean the loss of a lifetime's accumulated seniority.

As workers become older, they also show more interest in security rather than in economic rewards or the intrinsic satisfaction of the job. According to Eli Chinoy[78], 35 is the crucial age at which concern for security tends to dominate, and economic incentives have much less impact. General support for this view can be derived from a recent report on the extent of overtime and shift-working in the U.K.[79], since these represent the two major strategies by which low-skill employees can increase their earnings. Among the sample of over 1000 male manual workers aged 18 and over (drawn from Derby, Sheffield and North Kent), 87 per cent gave no reason other than pay for working overtime. There was a clear relationship between age and the amount of overtime worked, a peak being reached in the thirties, the age of a married couple with a growing family (77 per cent of workers in this age-group were found to work some overtime, 38 per cent more than ten hours each week). The majority of shiftworkers, moreover, appeared to be unskilled workers with dependent families, and the majority of those in jobs requiring shift operation had chosen such jobs because of the higher earnings.

Much of the same holds true at more senior management levels. Harry Roff's recent survey[80] of a small sample of senior executives argues strongly that the motivational value of money deteriorates markedly once the children have left school, and at the same time geographical mobility declines. "Moves tended to be expensive, disruptive of business and family life, and would quite often involve some unattractive features such as increased travel, difficult personal situ-

---

* L. G. Reynolds (*The Structure of Labour Markets*, Harper, 1951) says that, in general, the desire to change employment decreases after three years seniority and becomes negligible after ten years.

ations, and the inevitable risks of change. . . . The great majority of those interviewed had an interesting job, congenial colleagues, and quite often were happily settled in an area at home where there were community and other interests for themselves or their wives."

Equally, a study of loyalty in two factories[81] has showed that economic factors (high wages, bonuses, and incentives) predominated for those in their first two years of service but were gradually replaced by "organizational" factors (the friendly atmosphere, good relationships with superiors, etc.) as seniority increased. It seems that the longer a person remains with a single employer, the more likely it is that his work will cease to be purely a means of obtaining income and will develop into the basis of a good deal of his social life. There is also the further point that economic requirements normally decline as the individual becomes older.

SOCIAL FACTORS

Fear of disturbing interpersonal relationships is crucial in determining resistance to change and applies not only to the work situation but also to the wider socio-economic environment. People normally have to undergo a difficult initiation period at work before they develop satisfactory relationships with their colleagues, and they will oppose any transfer to a different job if this necessitates the disruption of existing social contacts and the effort of establishing new ones. Management is very often misguided, therefore, if it believes that employee morale will improve if workers are forcibly rotated between jobs in order allegedly to give variety. Enid Mumford's study[82] of a firm of baby-food manufacturers found that an exaggerated level of labour turnover among its female operators was partly due to the enforced movement of the girls between different tasks; her suggestion that work groups should be stabilized, so that satisfactory group relationships and loyalties could develop, led to a considerable improvement in the situation.

The disturbances of change also affect the precarious balance between the individual's own personality needs, his interpersonal relationships, and the requirements of the job. Over a period of time, the worker characteristically adjusts these three factors into a reasonably effective mix (if he does not, he is likely to leave the organization for a more congenial atmosphere; or he may simply become a deviant). Thus, for example, the man who wants to boss others around, even if he has no official authority, can generally manoeuvre himself into a position which enables him to initiate activity in others : he can become a car park attendant. Alterations in work procedures, however, may upset these laboriously built up arrangements. If the change is in the direction of automation, moreover, it often implies, as we have already seen, a considerable weakening of group structures in the workplace because employees tend to become specialists working in isolation rather than groups working as a team. It is true that such changes offer satisfactions of their own (such as the increased status as a specialist), but the period of transition is bound to involve some tension and resistance.

The worker's position in the community is equally important in structuring his response to technical changes which may alter his way of life because they introduce norms (like shift work) which are contrary to established norms, or which may even force the worker to leave his domicile and work elsewhere. D. Pecaut[83] has formulated three hypotheses which indicate the probability that attachment to community gives rise to negative behaviour whenever innovation is in the offing :

The stronger is the consciousness of community, the more difficult it is to accept technical change. In some cases, the prospect of change can arouse behaviour approximating to mutiny, in which non-workers reinforce the resistance of the workers themselves. Pecaut quotes the closure of the unprofitable mines in south-central France and the transfer of the miners to other locations, which was accompanied by violent opposition. Local tradesmen, elected representatives and parish priests reacted vigorously to what they imagined was a threat to the collectivity as a whole; many locals referred to the proposed transfer of miners as "deportation".

The more the working life is merged with life outside work in the community, the more difficult it is to accept technical change. As Pecaut points out, such merging often indicates that people's occupations were not "freely" chosen in the first place, since there were only one or two employers in the neighbourhood. This absence of alternatives is likely to produce resistance to all forms of innovation—whether occupational, geographical, or technological. Where people have entered jobs with minimal feelings of enthusiasm but with a stronge sense that the work is simply something from which there is no escape, they tend to hang on desperately to their occupational status as one of the few ways of gaining prestige within the community, and this must inevitably mean a root and branch preference for the status quo.

The more the new norms introduced by technical change are contrary to established norms, the more the change will be felt as something which cannot be assimilated. Shift work requires much more careful handling if it is being introduced in an area where shift operations are a comparative novelty, as distinct from places like Scunthorpe where at least a quarter of the male labour force are accustomed to shift systems.

The recent instance of an electronics company faced with the prospect of atrophy after the cancellation of Government contracts and other setbacks illustrates the potential advantages to be extracted from the conservatism and stability of rural areas. The firm's plants in North London were in a ferment of insecurity and erupted into stoppages, frequent exhibitions of union militancy, and wild rumours, while at the company's Gloucester location there were virtually no disturbances whatever. Among the factors contributing to this state of affairs were undoubtedly the confident feelings of continuity (based on many years' experience) among the staff, their favourable attitudes towards the firm, the team spirit within the plant, and the workers' high level of integration into the local community. In a study of warehouse performance in a company with 72 warehousing divisions throughout North America, storing and distributing pharmaceutical products, it was found that warehouses characterized by relatively low urbanization (small community, few employees, lower wages, absence of unions, and a lower proportion of male workers) were likely to show a superior performance, especially according to the financial and labour turnover indices[84].

Not surprisingly, most surveys of manpower mobility show that married individuals are less (geographically) mobile than single people, and that individuals with families are the least mobile of all*. This does not necessarily imply that the married man and the family man are resistant to technological innovation, except in so far as reluctance to

---

* To some extent, this declining mobility may be correlated with age, but it remains valid even for age-matched samples.

accept one form of change generally accompanies resistance to other types of change. Much depends, too, on the extent to which family life is inter-related with the man's working world. Resistance to change tends to be maximum where this inter-relationship is at its height—in a non-diversified community like a coal-mining village or fishing port. Pivotal questions of status, which the family normally derives from the occupational prestige of the breadwinner, may force him to respond negatively to proposed changes (like the introduction of shifts or a re-alignment of traditional skill differentials) that seem to threaten the whole family's position in society. In more diversified communities, status is much less dependent on occupation alone and therefore such considerations are less important.

Several authors[85] have suggested that resistance to change is stronger among women, although it is difficult to make precise comparisons because women normally work for shorter periods than men and are not the principal wage-earners in the household. Apart from geographical mobility, where women's reluctance to change is most pronounced, there are some factors which theoretically should enable women to accept change with comparative equanimity. It is known, for example, that women attach less importance to wages and economic incentives than men—their satisfaction at work is more likely to derive from the social relationships which it offers—and provided the proposed change does not disturb these relationships their reaction will not generally be hostile*. Moreover, women can face the prospect of technological unemployment, especially if they are married and their husbands work;

---

* Like most other generalizations about human behaviour, this statement needs to be treated with reservation. A. Hunt ("Women in Employment", *Ministry of Labour Gazette*, May 1966) found that for women the principal attractions in going to work were, in descending order of importance, financial; for company; to dispel boredom; to obtain independence. Wild and his colleagues, in a survey of hourly-paid female operatives, submit that "The distinctive difference between our satisfied and dissatisfied subjects lay in the lack of self-actualization perceived by the latter in relation to their work . . . Lack of fulfilment of these needs may lead to dissatisfaction, frustration and withdrawal from the work situation." On the other hand, Wild has to admit that of the 355 individuals in the sample, only a proportion, approximately 30 per cent, was dissatisfied—yet they were all doing objectively the same job. See R. Wild, A. B. Hill and C. C. Ridgeway, "Job Satisfaction and Labour Turnover Amongst Women Workers", *Journal of Management Studies*, Vol. 7 (1), February 1970, 78–86.

most women are white-collar workers for whom, in any case, technological unemployment is not a real fear; and finally, women find it
easier to identify with the aims of management.

The inescapable conclusion arising out of this lengthy discussion is
that resistance to change tends to focus on the human relations and
social problems generated by the change rather than on the technical
aspects. As Sayles and Strauss remark, "It is not change itself which
causes the resistance, but the meaning of the change for the people
involved."* People oppose innovation if their social relationships, their
status or their security are threatened, and those introducing change
must pay more attention to these considerations if tension and conflict
are to be minimized. This particularly applies to technical specialists,
who tend to under-estimate the social implications of change either
because they are totally preoccupied with their specialism, or because
they are so convinced of the logical superiority of their innovations that
they regard all opposition as ignorance, stubbornness and stupidity. The
introduction of computers is a situation which often exemplifies this
tendency. The basically sound ideas of the systems designers may be
destroyed or damaged because they do not understand the human
beings who have to operate the system. Sometimes they make over-
simplified and unrealistic assumptions in their models of the way in
which reality operates. Yet it is interesting that specialists of this kind,
though eager to propose changes elsewhere, can resist change as
enthusiastically as anyone else when it comes to their own work.

SUMMARY

1.   Resistance to change is partially offset by the desire for new
experiences or a break from routine.

2.   A change regarded as trivial by management may be regarded as
anything but trivial to the people affected directly by the change.

* L. R. Sayles and G. Strauss, *Human Behaviour in Organizations*, Prentice-
Hall, 1966, 303. See also D. Pecaut, "The Worker and the Community", in
Ref. 83, p. 121: "The individual sees the consequences of change, not so much
at the level of the firm as at the level of his social existence as a whole, his family
life and his community life."

3. Management's assumptions about resistance to change tend to be a self-fulfilling prophecy : by assuming in advance that (and then behaving as if) employees will resist all changes put before them, management "causes" the very behaviour which they anticipated in the first place.

4. Intelligent high-grade employees will not necessarily accept change any more enthusiastically than manual workers.

5. Resistance to change has positive aspects, e.g., by forcing the advocates of change to consider their arguments more carefully.

6. The successful introduction of change is easier to accomplish in organizations which frequently undergo the change process, since their employees become accustomed to an equilibrium position incorporating change itself, as distinct from organizations where change is a relatively infrequent (and thus traumatic) phenomenon.

7. Individuals resist change if they perceive the change as a threat to their existing or anticipated level of need-satisfaction.

8. Belongingness needs are especially significant in that productivity and other indices of performance are likely to deteriorate if employees feel that their opportunities for social interaction are endangered.

9. Automation is often interpreted as a threat to job security and status, particularly among manual and lower-level white-collar workers —and it seems likely that these fears are justified.

10. Change promotes conflict if only because it increases the flow of orders, thereby sharpening control over subordinates who may like to think of themselves as autonomous.

11. Introducing change by means of orders is dangerous because, when people are *told* to change, they tend to become stubborn, hostile, and defensive.

12. Employees may even oppose changes in job design aimed at creating more interest in the work, if they have already acclimatized themselves to the performance of routine tasks.

13. On the other hand, there is strong evidence to support the view that the re-introduction of human decision-making into jobs otherwise mechanized, can be highly effective in improving performance.

14. Good communication cannot *eliminate* resistance to change, if only because the mere provision of facts cannot dispel the individual's anxieties about how *he* will react to the change.

15. Factual information about change is only effective if it anticipates the questions in the minds of employees, and answers these questions before rumour has a chance to gain a foothold.

16. Willingness to be occupationally and geographically mobile decreases markedly with accumulating seniority.

17. The employee's reaction to change is conditioned additionally by his relationship to the external community in which the organization operates, and also by any perceived threat to his status in the family.

18. "It is not change itself which causes the resistance, but the meaning of the change for the people involved." (L. R. Sayles and G. Strauss.)

CHAPTER 4

Hierarchical Variations in Attitudes to Change

PEOPLE on the shop floor tend to be more resistant to organizational change than members of management, probably for a combination of reasons[86]. First, their work is more tightly programmed and thus their scope for decision-making is more limited. Manual workers are frequently told not only what they are to do, but also how to do it (in precise detail). They are likely to view proposed innovations as a possible threat to the modest (and therefore highly important) amount of self-control and discretion they have been able to extract. As John Nelson-Jones[87] notes, too, "The inevitable element of constraint in factory work is particularly galling for workers living in a democratic permissive and relatively affluent society. The factory atmosphere is in conflict with the values of the larger society of which the factory is a part. The worker is in much the same position as a private in the army and knows it. Not only is his work trivial but he is at the bottom of a chain of command. In many cases the twin blow to his self-esteem is too great to be shrugged off."

Secondly, because the work of industrial operatives tends to encourage social interaction (more than that of managers), they are likely to become more committed to formal routines and customary patterns of behaviour. As a result they see the sustained observance of these routines as closely linked to their interests as individuals, and naturally they oppose change if it disturbs these cherished practices.

A third factor is that blockages to upward promotion (a feature of most shop floor jobs) also tend to encourage the formation of close cohesive ties between operatives. Elsewhere, Lupton explains that "Because of the demand for new skills, educational opportunity is

63

widened and it now becomes possible, for example, for the manual worker to see for his son a possibility of a professional career."[88] It is worth noting, however, that Lupton says nothing about the chances of upward mobility for the manual worker himself. "The fact that mobility has become increasingly institutionalized via the educational system means that while there may be increased changes of intergenerational mobility through education, the chances of intra-generational mobility through work are declining. To enter a factory job with a secondary modern education is to take a job that is more and more a life sentence."[89]

A recent article[90] has drawn attention to some of the long-term effects of technological innovation on promotion opportunities at lower occupational levels. The findings confirmed the observations of earlier writers that "change in process technology is accompanied by increased management stress on formal educational credentials." In addition, technological advances are accompanied by "decreased promotional opportunities for lower-level employees" and, not unnaturally, "increased problems revolving around attracting and retaining personnel for lower level managerial positions."[91] These posts are becoming less attractive not only because they are perceived as "dead-end" positions but also because of the changing nature of the work performed and the inadequate compensation.

Manual workers may feel, much more than white-collar employees, that promotion would cause them social problems at home and at work. In a survey comparing the attitudes of clerical and manual workers in the same Scottish company towards three aspects of their working lives (promotion, trade unionism, the company and its management), A. J. M. Sykes[92] found that manual workers rejected upward social mobility, and therefore promotion, for this reason. It is of course possible that such rejection of promotion opportunities is simply a rationalization of the fact that very few such opportunities exist, particularly in view of the high value placed upon upward mobility by the clerks in the survey. Yet at the same time, given the extremely small likelihood of advancement beyond operative level, it is scarcely surprising that manual workers exhibit a higher degree of frustration than office employees, as measured by "indicators of frustration" like looking for another job, wanting to stir up trouble, clock watching, and feelings of depression.

Not only are shop-floor workers more resistant to change, for the reasons just outlined, but managers are more likely to welcome it. For one thing, managers are generally better educated than manual workers and there is a very high correlation between level of education and all forms of mobility, whether geographical, occupational, and technical. It seems that the experience of higher education enables the individual to develop specific expectations and wider career possibilities, both of which encourage geographical mobility. Since geographical mobility is almost always found alongside the willingness to accept technical change, managers are seldom opponents of innovation. Furthermore, the higher a manager is placed in the hierarchical structure of an organization, the more probable it is that he will recognize and accept the need for change and at the same time identify his own future with that of the company. As there are far fewer managers than non-managers, and as many firms have declared policies of promotion from within wherever possible, opportunities available to managers to move from employer to employer are often considerably less than for shop-floor workers. This means that the senior manager is more likely to accept change in the short term, even when it is against his personal wishes, whilst he explores alternative opportunities elsewhere. Finally, managers tend to live in a less-localized social environment than shop-floor workers, and characteristically travel several miles to work. All these observations support the generalization that *the higher the level in the hierarchy, the less is the resistance to change*[93].

There are even different degrees of opposition to change among manual workers, largely related to the status of the work itself. L. R. Sayles[94] describes four basic types of manual work. "Apathetic" and "Erratic" workers are the relatively low-skilled and low-paid groups (e.g., drill press operators) whereas "Strategic" and "Conservative" workers enjoy higher status, are more highly skilled and earn better wages (e.g., wire-drawers and printers). "The most discouraging aspect of the position of the Apathetic and Erratic groups in the plant is the likelihood that they will provide the most serious opposition to technological change. Although the Apathetics offer minimum open challenges to management, their attitude, and that of the Erratics, is a blind resistance to what is new and different. The lack the internal organization and structure which would provide them with the capacity for change."[95] In this country, the Liverpool study of the steel industry found attitudes towards technical change to be "clearly related to occupational structure". The degree of approval "declines as one descends the occupational hierarchy; the higher the status of a group, and the greater its interest in the present organization of production, the more positive is its attitude."[96]

Yet there is some evidence for the belief that if employees bring nothing more than an *instrumental* attitude to their work, they will exhibit comparatively little resistance to change. An instrumental approach to employment exists if workers are interested in work not as an end in itself but merely as a means to achieving ends that lay outside the work situation. Goldthorpe[97] argues that the car workers in his sample had an almost exclusively instrumental orientation towards their jobs. It is emphasized, moreover, that these instrumental attitudes were not a reaction to the arduous and tedious nature of work on the assembly line. The men involved had become car assemblers precisely because of the high wages prevailing in the industry. They had chosen economic rewards above any intrinsic satisfactions that might be obtained from work, a point which is substantiated by Clack[98] : "complaints were most numerous and vigorous when the tracks stopped moving—and the much lower 'waiting-time' rates of pay applied. No one spoke of such pauses providing a breathing space to offset monotony, exhaustion, or emotional strain; the level of earnings seemed the major concern."

One would perhaps expect that such men, if not primarily committed to the job as such, would not resist change so long as their incomes were guaranteed. If they do oppose changes, therefore, it is very probably because they fear that their earnings will be threatened. This is especially true if the men are on piecework or other economic incentives. So far as car workers are concerned, fear of insecurity (clearly connected with income) is a very important factor in producing resistance to innovation, although Clack points out that such workers will tolerate "an acceptable level of insecurity . . . resentment became vociferous or active only when this level increased sharply."[99]

It has been suggested that the high earnings of workers in the British car industry are a major form of compensation for a degree of irregularity and insecurity of employment, and that car workers bargain aggressively in good times to make up for "losses" in bad times[100]. This notion certainly seems logical and plausible, given the insecurity endemic in the industry, and it fits in with the workers' expressed attitudes.

If the worker is only interested in the monetary rewards associated with his work, then, his resistance to change is likely to be minimal so long as certain fundamental requirements are fulfilled. "Whatever the type of organization or the method of introduction, an organizational change which does not affect the wage level or basic working conditions of the uninvolved individual will be accepted."[101] This generalization appears relevant, for example, to "certain married women working part-time in industrial jobs." On the other hand, "The possession by the workforce of an instrumental attitude to work does not give the employer licence to impose what constraints he likes on them. If, for example, the management attempted to make its control over work activities tighter and more stringent, then, despite their instrumental orientation, the workers' attitudes and behaviour might well become less impervious to the nature of the work situation."[102]

SUMMARY

1.   Resistance to change is inversely correlated with the individual's hierarchical level within the organization.

2.   Decreased promotion opportunities for low-level employees may create more frustration and resentment among such workers or alternatively may generate more effective rationalizing mechanisms in which the desire for advancement is rejected in favour of other aims.

3.   If employees hold a predominantly instrumental attitude towards their work, they are less likely to resist technological changes so long as their earnings and security are not threatened.

CHAPTER 5

Organizational and Psychological Factors

IF AN organization is to cope with change successfully, it must have a significant proportion of employees with personality characteristics associated with flexibility. Whether such individuals are present in sufficient numbers will depend very largely on the nature of the organization itself. As Pym argues, "Individuals are attracted to concerns with a similar climate of beliefs."[103]

In turn, the character of the organization is likely to be influenced by the frequency with which, in the past, the organization has had to respond to large-scale environmental changes or has felt the need to innovate for itself. Plausibly, therefore, organizations noted for the security of tenure which they offer and the stability of the work-functions performed will attract employees motivated by the desire for security and stability, qualities clearly associated with personal rigidity and resistance to innovation. In short, mechanistic or bureaucratic structures tend to emphasize the recruitment of fairly inflexible personalities, partly because the personnel operation is unconsciously oriented in favour of people who will "fit into" the existing organizational climate, and partly because the overwhelming majority of applications to join such organizations are likely to be from individuals with mechanistic personalities.

Rapid change in these organizations is then hampered by the kinds of people who have been recruited into them. Lupton shows, for example, how the patterns of control in large organizations are dependent on tight formal structures and reporting procedures. "These, in turn, tend to induce the apathetic 'I-won't-do-more-than-I-have-to' attitude, the empire-building, the sub-optimization, and the rat-racing, which characterize large-scale bureaucracy and the 'resistance to change' it exhibits. This kind of organization is likely to be anything but flexible and adaptive, because the structure places a premium on defensive play-safe untrusting people. It is not as if people are inherently defensive, etc., it is the organization that makes them so."[104]

Apart from the limited flexibility imposed on bureaucracies by the kind of personalities attracted to employment in them[105], there is a wealth of descriptive and research literature dealing with the organizational problems experienced by bureaucracies in situations where fairly rapid change is required. In general, it appears that a rigid system of administration enforced during a period of change is likely to produce low efficiency, low productivity, high labour turnover, and increased absenteeism, although the precise reaction will depend very strongly on the cultural acceptance of bureaucratic forms. In more democratic and permissive societies, the authoritarian climate of bureaucracies generates hostilities and dysfunctional conflicts that tend to be particularly violent during periods of change.

Representative of the available published research on bureaucracy is Michel Crozier's *The Bureaucratic Phenomenon*[106]. Like most other writers on the subject, Crozier emphasizes the rigidity of bureaucratic structures and suggests that "a system of organization whose main characteristic is its rigidity will not adjust easily to change and will tend to resist change as much as possible." Perhaps the principal effect of this rigidity is that it prevents the organization from drawing appropriate conclusions from its mistakes. Indeed, Crozier defines "bureaucratic organization" as "an organization that cannot correct its behaviour by learning from its errors."[107] Much organizational change is in practice prompted by the need to rectify faults which have come to light through the constant feedback of information. In some organizations, this process functions efficiently (or relatively so). In bureaucracies, the feedback process of error–information–correction does not function well, and so there cannot be any quick readjustment of programmes of action in the light of errors committed. On the contrary, if a bureaucratic rule seems to be inadequate in dealing with a particular case, this does not generate pressure to abandon the rule but rather initiates efforts to make the rule "more complete, more precise, and more binding". The same process occurs not only in industrial organizations but also in the central activity of government itself : the rigid policies of technologically-advanced societies reflect the fact that once the decision-making apparatus has disgorged a policy it becomes very difficult to change it. "The alternative to the status quo is the prospect of repeating the whole anguishing process of arriving at decisions. This explains to some extent the curious phenomenon that decisions taken with enormous doubt and perhaps with a close division become practically sacrosanct once adopted. The whole administrative machinery swings behind their implementation as if activity could still all doubts."[108]

A further complication is that bureaucracies are, by definition, highly centralized. Change could be accomplished in a gradual and constant process if potential decisions about prospective changes could be made by officials located sufficiently near to the operating levels of the organization. But "a bureaucratic organization does not allow for such initiative at the lower echelons; decisions must be made where power is located, i.e., on top."[109] Yet this fact makes a "permanent adjustment" policy impracticable, if only because failures in upward communication systems prevent advance warnings from getting to the top. Even when the top echelons do hear of a situation which appears to require alteration, they will have difficulty in making a decision because of the accumulated pressures of impersonal rules also needing amendment. This means that "a bureaucratic system will resist change as long as it can; it will move only when serious dysfunctions develop and no other alternatives remain."

In addition, bureaucracies adjust to change in a very peculiar way, by applying a universalistic solution to the whole structure, even to areas where dysfunctions are not seriously felt. "The essential rhythm prevalent in such organizations is, therefore, an alternation of long periods of stability with very short periods of crisis and change." Indeed, "Crisis is a distinctive and necessary element of the bureaucratic system. It provides the only means of making the necessary adjustments, and it therefore plays a role in enabling the organization to develop and, indirectly, for centralization and impersonality to grow." Change in bureaucracies is always "a deeply felt crisis" for the three principal reasons already discussed : the inevitable delays before any change can be initiated, the amplitude of the change when it does occur, and the intense resistance it must overcome because of the personality types involved. Crozier concludes that "a bureaucratic system of organization is not only a system that does not correct its behaviour in view of its errors; it is also *too rigid to adjust without crisis to the transformations that the accelerated evolution of industrial society makes more and more imperative.*" (Author's italics.)

If organizations are to cope with change without acute disruption, they must increase the amount of flexibility inherent in the structure, at least during the period of the change as such. In the terminology previously employed, this means moving out of an existing equilibrium into a phase of disequilibrium before a new equilibrium is reached. Thus "a process of disorganization is often necessary before a change can be integrated into a restructured and re-adapted operating system."[110] According to Kurt Lewin, "A successful change includes three aspects : unfreezing the present level, moving to a new level and freezing group life on the new level. Since any level is determined by a force field, permanency implies that the new force field is made relatively secure against change."[111]

It is worth noting the prediction that organizations of the future will be permanently unfrozen (or organic). According to Warren Bennis, "They will be adaptive rapidly-changing *temporary systems*, organized around problems to be solved by groups of relative strangers with diverse professional skills. The group will be arranged on organic rather than mechanical models; they will evolve in response to problems rather than to programmed expectations . . . Adaptive problem-solving, temporary systems of diverse specialists linked together by co-ordinating executives in an organic flux—this is the organizational form that will gradually replace bureaucracy."[112] Some companies have already experimented successfully along these lines with project groups, matrix structures combining several functional or product groups, and so on*. These types of structure—likely to be found in aerospace, research and development organizations—have an incidental spin-off for the status

---

* For further details, see C. J. Middleton, "How to Set Up a Project Organization", *Harvard Business Review*, Vol. 45 (2), March–April 1967, 73–82; J. F. Mee, "Matrix Organization", *Business Horizons*, Vol. 7 (2), Summer 1964, 70–72.

of the Personnel Manager in that he becomes more directly part of a team rather than being stigmatized on the staff side of the staff/line dichotomy.

There is a case for saying that once the need for change has been established, the change itself should be implemented as rapidly as possible, at whatever organizational and personal cost. Individuals then have to undergo no more than a single well-defined trauma before the return to normality (or equilibrium) can begin, whereas the gradual introduction of changes implies an artificially-prolonged period of confusion, uncertainty, and insecurity for many of the participants. If a change is introduced slowly enough, it may not be noticed at all, or the organization may become accustomed to constant gradual change (as in the fashion industry). On the other hand, if the change is so gradual that people fail to realize it has occurred, they may still continue to behave in ways appropriate to the old situation. Also, slow change creates anxieties of its own; employees begin to think that "something is happening, but we don't know what" and exaggerated fears arise about where the change is leading.

In practice the arguments are finely balanced. The consultants called in to advise Geest Industries in 1970 felt that "basically, it is a matter of temperament—whether you dive head first into the water, or go in one toe at a time."[113] Circumstances dictated the former strategy, since the 1970 banana crop was hit first by drought, then by a dock strike, then by a hurricane. There was a fire at the main banana distribution depot, and a postal strike caused severe losses to Geest's mail-order bulb and plant business. This experience put Geest in a suitable frame of mind to accept rapid action, although it is probable that, without the crisis of 1970, the company would have simply put off indefinitely the tensions and discomforts of large-scale reorientation. In Lester's view, "Even if everything doesn't work first time round, competent managers are likely to learn more about their business in the process of trying than if the reform is spread over a much longer period."

To talk in mechanistic and organic terms is to infer that organizations are entirely free to choose the degree of flexibility to be adopted at any given time. In fact, there are several important determinants of the organization structure. These major factors are considered in detail below.

THE TECHNOLOGY EMPLOYED

Technology can be defined (as some American sociologists, such as Dubin, have done) by dividing it into two major phases. First, it implies the tools, instruments, machines, plants, and technical formulae basic to the performance of any work. Secondly, technology means a body of ideas which express the goals of the work, its functional importance, and the rationale of the methods employed. Woodward[114] has concentrated on the "operations technology" of manufacturing organizations, referring to the equipping and sequencing of activities in an organization's workflow, whereas Perrow[115] discusses "materials technology", namely, the characteristics of the physical and informational materials used by the organization. Perrow argues that the degree of stability in the nature of material employed, and the extent to which routine codifiable techniques ("analysable search") can be applied to them, influence the way in which work roles can be defined.

Repetitive, routine and predictable operations are susceptible to tighter programming—and, therefore, a more highly centralized form of control—than organizations designed to cope with weather irregularities or where constant creativity is essential. Joan Woodward's work has shown that technologies can be broadly classified according to the controllability and predictability of the production process. Units made to customers' orders (as in bespoke tailoring) are highly unpredictable, whereas flow production (as in oil refineries) is highly predictable.

It appears from her research, by virtue of the quantity of written communications in mass-production firms, that the organization of such firms was less flexible than the other two types. This could perhaps be coupled with the fact that managers in mass-production firms spent much of their time coping with crises of all kinds. Faced with the requirement to restore equilibrium with the least possible delay, it is scarcely surprising that mass production managers resorted to authoritarian methods. One of the main drawbacks to the participative approach is that democratic procedures and consultation take time which the organization may feel it can scarcely afford. Organizations where these conditions exist, therefore, are likely to remain authoritarian and bureaucratic even when rapid innovation is essential. Process industries can accommodate themselves more adequately to the problems of change simply because they have more time to do so.

A. K. Rice[116] has produced considerable supporting evidence for the importance of technology in the chemical industry. He points out that in the typical chemical plant, much of the space is occupied by equipment in which cooling, settling, or other processes are going on without human interference. Each part of the process has an intrinsic momentum which, once started, is difficult to stop. Employees must accept the limitations imposed by such production methods, although Rice suggests that the discipline of a physical process is easier to tolerate than the discipline derived from human authority, which is often unstable, authoritarian, and erratic.

More recent evidence has cast some doubt on the legitimacy of technology as a determinant of organization structures. As Child[117] has argued, the work itself (its planning, arrangement, and meaning for those concerned) may well be an organizational variable of more significance than technology, although the two concepts are bound to be linked. Hage and Aiken[118], too, have translated technology into "routineness of work". And, even if technology still remains a major influence on structural patterns within organizations, the relationship (as with environment) is by no means deterministic. The work of the Tavistock Institute suggests the scope for considerable organizational choice to suit the preferences of employees within a given technological framework[119]. Job enrichment also implies a manipulation of the structure to suit human capabilities and potential, while the basic technology remains constant[120].

THE FORM OF ACCOUNTABILITY OF THE ORGANIZATION

It is possible that a technical college with a pre-determined budget on whose spending it must report to the local authority will control its staff more closely than a private business whose accountability to shareholders is looser and more intermittent. If this is true, it may be attributable as much to the personalities involved as to the forms of accountability employed. We have already seen that people are attracted to organizations with a similar climate of beliefs. It is not implausible that most people attracted to technical college work (particularly those who demonstrate sufficient conformity to attain positions of seniority and authority) are deficiency-motivated, security-conscious authoritarians. Such individuals will tend to apply close "job-centred" forms of control over their subordinates as a matter of preference, dictated by their rigid personalities and bureaucratic environment in general, rather than by the form of accountability alone.

THE SIZE OF THE ORGANIZATION

The principal effect of increasing size is an inevitable increase in the number of administrative levels in the organization, and this has important implications both for the structure and for the behaviour of the employees in the structure. "When sufficiently large samples are taken, the behaviour of those who work in the big unit, whether judged by risk of accident, sickness, dispute, or absence without leave, displays less evidence of attachment to their colleagues than does the behaviour of those who work in the small. The estrangement of the individual from his work increases as the unit he serves gets bigger."[121] As Revans demonstrates, the larger organization is less efficient according to several criteria, whether one is examining the number of deaths in hospitals; absenteeism, turnover, and output rates in factories; strikes in coal mines; or sales volume per employee in retail establishments. It is possible that this suggests some industrial counterpart to Arnold Toynbee's thesis about the failure of civilizations. Such failures invariably seem to be heralded by those twin products of bigness, namely, stagnating authority and deadening standardization. Both Plato and Aristotle recognized the existence of an optimum size for the city state. Plato's *Laws* limited the ideal city to 5040 citizens and Aristotle's *Politics* mentions a maximum of 10 000. In each case it was argued that good laws are virtually impossible to formulate in an over-populated state, that is, one where direct democracy has to be replaced by indirect representative methods. Size alone is not the offending factor, but rather the structural and operating changes brought about by size.

Blau[122] has produced data suggesting that increased size generates structural differentiation within organizations, and that this differentiation in turn enlarges the absolute (although not the relative) size of an organization's administrative component. As the number of administrative levels proliferates, more opportunities are created for "noise" to occur in the communication system. Messages both upward and downward may be distorted or even obliterated completely, with harmful effects on morale and efficiency. Supporting evidence for this view derives from Worthy's study of Sears Roebuck[123] in which he concluded that "flat" organizations are preferable to "tall" structures in terms of employee morale and performance.

Equally, Porter and Lawler, investigating the satisfaction experienced by managers in companies of different sizes and structures, found that "flat" structures gave greater feelings of self-actualization whereas managers in "tall" organizations emphasized the value of security[124].

This evidence is undoubtedly consonant with the earlier observation that organizations tend to attract individuals with a similar climate of beliefs, since bureaucratic structures are typically "tall" (the archetypal example is the British Civil Service) and set great store by the degree of security they offer. "Flat" structures, by contrast, with relatively few administrative levels, presuppose a substantial measure of decentralization and delegation, which are known to be organizational characteristics conducive to the willing initiation and rapid assimilation of change (because they remove the necessity for those critical delays before a decision on change is taken at a sufficiently senior level).

Bernard Indik[125] has discussed the effects of increasing size on organizational behaviour from another point of view. With larger units, there is a greater need for co-ordination and supervision, and this involves the introduction of more impersonal controls, known to be less effective than interpersonal controls in attracting potential members to the organization. Indik argues that "the less attracted to the organization the members are, the more they will tend to leave the organization both temporarily (absence) and permanently (turnover)." With increasing size, too, there is a tendency towards narrower role specialization. Jobs become less complex and therefore less satisfying to perform. Job enrichment and other similar approaches offer a partial solution, but the core of the problem lies in the organizational implications of sheer size.

A grim dilemma for the larger technologically-based corporations concerns the difficulty of maintaining a high rate of profitable product innovation, given that the established structure of such organizations— where ideas are proposed at a low level but disposed at a high level —militates against innovation. The equivalent problem for smaller organizations is how to retain, once they become large, the initial drive and dynamism which set them on the road to expansion in the first place.

A popular device among such organizations for coping with the uncertainties of technological and marketing innovations is to allow other (smaller) organizations to initiate these changes. Then, if the innovation is successful, the large organization can simply purchase the small, on the theoretical assumption that the benefits and financial returns created by the innovation will be transferred *in toto* to its new owners. Robert Heller[126] calls this process the "Lestoil Syndrome", after a once-obscure New Jersey detergent firm which began to bottle its heavy-duty industrial detergent and sell it to housewives. As sales soared, Lestoil's massive competitors "reacted with multi-million dollar force, swamping Lestoil in a sea of green bubbles." In Britain, Alexander Duckham was the first concern to produce a multi-grade lubricating oil for cars, doubling its turnover in four years until it had about one quarter of the United Kingdom market. However, the giants finally retaliated, Duckham's growth and profits fell until finally the whole company was purchased by British Petroleum—another victim of the Lestoil Syndrome.

As Donald A. Schon[127] remarks, large organizations prefer to deal in carefully-calculated risks rather than in the vague uncertainties of many potential commercial propositions. One way out of these difficulties is artificially to reduce the size of the enterprise so that entrepreneurial qualities of drive, independence, and dedication have a greater chance of showing themselves. This can be done by throwing out subsidiary offshoots or by the relatively new process of "venture management"[128] whereby a young executive is handed a project or a product (although at the early stage it may be nothing more than a raw idea) and told that it is his job to fashion it into a profitable business. At Du Pont, for example, the Venture Manager must first be convinced of the commercial viability of a proposed product by finding favourable answers to three questions :

(1)   Will it provide a satisfactory return on investment?

(2)   Will patent protection justify the risk?

(3)   Is the potential business large enough for the effort needed?

Once these points are satisfactorily established, skilled people from marketing, manufacturing, and research are transferred to work under the Venture Manager on a full-time basis, so that the group resembles a company in miniature and develops a strong vested interest in the success of its project. Using techniques of this kind Du Pont has marketed Crolyn, a new form of high-fidelity magnetic tape based on chromium dioxide rather than the usual iron oxide. Other companies employing Venture Management include Union Carbide and Minnesota Mining and Manufacturing. Broadly speaking, Venture Management appears to be successful because it overcomes the formidable obstacles deriving from the scientist's inability to see the commercial value of a new product or technological innovation, and the commercial departments' lack of interest in an idea which does not originate with them (the Them/Us conflict once again). Moreover, the companies using Venture Management claim that it attracts men of high potential, "not only because of the financial incentive and organizational advancement but—more important—because of the pride of accomplishment that comes when the venture is successful."[129]

THE EFFECTS OF THE ENVIRONMENT

No organization can afford to ignore the environment in which it operates, but organizations do vary with regard to their dependence on changes in the environment. As Sadler and Barry[130] put it, "an organization cannot evolve or develop in ways which merely reflect the goals, motives, or needs of its members or of its leadership, since it must always bow to the constraints imposed on it by the nature of its relationship with the environment." One particularly relevant phenomenon is environmental stress[131], defined as the degree of threat that faces the organization in the achievement of its goals, from external competition, hostility, or even indifference. Khandwalla suggests ways in which the organization may respond to increasing illiberality in the environment. For example, if the attainment of pluralistic goals is threatened, the overriding aim of survival may come to supersede all other considerations, the result being centralized decision-making and tighter controls*.

On the other hand, the environment is not totally outside the control

* One example concerns the way in which, for a time, any expenditure exceeding £25 had to receive the formal authorization of the Board in Lesney Products during the company's financial crisis of 1970.

of the organization. Managers may be free to choose, within defined constraints, the types of environment—markets, products, employee recruitment, and so on—in which they will operate. Galbraith[132] has drawn attention to the fact that the large business corporation can hope to manipulate and even create the demand for its goods and services. These arguments must supply an important element of qualification to suggestions of environmental determinism.

A "NATURAL" TENDENCY, NOTED BY BURNS AND STALKER, FOR ORGANIZATIONS TO DRIFT IN A BUREAUCRATIC OR CONSERVATIVE DIRECTION

As organizations expand, their operating procedures and controls become more formal and impersonal, thereby taking on the characteristics of bureaucracy. Weber did not believe that these features would normally be present in small organizations, and more recent research lends strong support to his hypothesis. For example, Pugh and his colleagues[133] found larger size to be the most powerful predictor of higher values on their structural factor related to the bureaucratic dimensions of specialization, use of procedures, and reliance on paperwork.

It may be that those with established positions in the structure have an "investment" in their statuses and are unlikely to encourage any alteration which could threaten the existing distribution of power, particularly when power is mainly determined by age and experience. Both these factors are strongly correlated with conservatism.

On the other hand, awareness of possible moves towards bureaucratization may consciously provoke attempts to counteract the trend. The Managing Director of Scot Meat Products[134] has said that "We are frustrated with the way we are drifting towards becoming the normal type of company, which we don't want to be." In Scot Meat Products, as in other firms with similar records of growth, the price of expansion has been the injection of middle-management levels acting as a barrier between the entrepreneurial originators of the company and the shop-floor employees. At the same time, the number of layers in the structure has been kept to a minimum (and it is notable that a "flat" organization is characteristic of the organic company). Senior management continuously promotes the philosophy that everything about the firm should be the interest and responsibility of everyone, regardless of rank. Unfortunately, increasing size is likely to make this "unitary"[135] approach—with one focus of loyalty and the absence of conflict—seem rather idealistic, if not Utopian. External observers may be tempted to conclude that, in practice, the "pluralistic" frame of reference would be more realistic at Scot Meat Products, in view of the spread of trade union activity and the reluctance of many employees to identify themselves with the company by purchasing shares, even at discount prices.

So far as individual characteristics and attitudes to change are concerned, substantial evidence is available regarding the personality attributes associated with effective and less effective performance in conditions of change. Denis Pym[136] has published the results of seven detailed studies into the responses of such occupational groups as young workers, female operatives engaged in manufacturing sports wear, electronic maintenance engineers, professional employees, marketing men, personnel in data-processing units, and managers. The Table summarizes Pym's assessment of the individual and managerial characteristics associated with effective (or ineffective) performance in conditions of change. Various procedures were used to obtain these data, principally the evaluations of superiors and subordinates of the managers concerned.

It is fair to add that not all the evidence substantiates Pym's hypothesis concerning the relationship between individual personality and attitudes to change. In a wide-ranging study on the effects of bureaucratic organization on the bureaucrat, Melvin Kohn[137] found that "men working in bureaucratic firms or organizations tend to value, not conformity, but self-direction. They are more open-minded . . . and are more receptive to change than are men who work in non-bureaucratic organizations. They show greater flexibility in dealing both with perceptual and with ideational problems. They spend their leisure time in more intellectually demanding activities." Furthermore, Kohn could not establish any special evidence for the social psychological characteristics associated with bureaucratization among employees of government and non-profit organizations as compared with employees of equally bureaucratized profit-making firms. Kohn even submits the possibility that "bureaucracies may hold a special attraction for self-directed intellectually-flexible men who are receptive to innovation and change". The features of bureaucracy likely to prove appealing to such men include the fact that bureaucracy offers more complex jobs than

TABLE 1

INDIVIDUAL AND MANAGERIAL CHARACTERISTICS ASSOCIATED WITH MORE
AND LESS SUCCESSFUL PERFORMANCE IN ORGANIZATIONAL CHANGE.

Less successful	Individual characteristics	More successful
Towards equilibrium Deficiency motivated, concern for safety and security Preoccupation with means	Orientation	Towards growth Enthusiasm for change, desire for new experiences, risk taking Greater attention to ends
Belief in a 'one best way'	Sentiments	Openness to more than one course of action
Regularity/order, financial security, prestige/status	Work aspirations	Freedom to be responsible, concern for achievement, interesting work
Limited and conventional	Leisure interests	More diverse and less conventional
	Managerial characteristics	
Boss is the 'expert' on subordinate's job	View of technical skills	Boss no longer expects to be, nor is regarded as, the 'expert'
Efficiency and human relations are separate features of behaviour	View of dimensions of leadership	Efficiency and human relations are merged
Submissive	Relations with superiors	Equality in relations with others, authority according to contribution
Directive and authoritative	Relations with subordinates	
Decisions are of a serial kind, i.e. based upon assumptions that previously successful solutions can be applied to new problems	Decision making	Less dependence on experience and more on the evaluation of the evidence

other comparable organizations, although individuals have to operate under rather closer supervision; they work under an externally-imposed pressure of time that results in their having to think faster; they work a shorter week, in the company of, but not necessarily in harness with, co-workers; they face greater competition; they enjoy much greater job protection and security; and they may earn more than other men of similar educational background.

Nevertheless, Kohn's findings have to be treated with considerable reserve. His correlations were very small (although significant), a fact which itself may be revealing if it means that bureaucracy exerts a much smaller psychological impact than has been assumed by writers like Merton[138]. Moreover, it is questionable whether the results reflect bureaucratization or merely size, or technology, or both. Finally, the research methodology itself may have been responsible for producing structured results. The respondents' receptiveness or resistance to innovation and change was indexed by responses to such questions as "Are you generally one of the first people to try out something new, or do you wait until you see how it's worked out for other people?" and by agreement or disagreement with statements like "It generally works out best to keep on doing things the way they have been done before."

Pym argues strongly that "the belief that there is 'only one best way of doing most things' is a useful predictor of the individual's *inability* to cope with change." Yet this belief in the "one best way" is an assumption underlying much early management theory and it is still highly influential. In support of this view Pym repeats a Joan Woodward anecdote[139] concerning the unusual organization structure of a successful firm in which 30 departmental supervisors reported indiscriminately to five senior executives. The system appeared to work well, and 28 of the supervisors endorsed this impression. The remaining two, however, disagreed and said they would be much happier if responsible to one person only; they talked a lot about the "unity of command" principle. *Both had taken the Diploma in Management Studies and were much more organization-conscious than their colleagues, none of whom had any formal management training.* "They had definite ideas about what was right and wrong in the organization and much of their discontent arose from comparing their own situation with what they thought was the ideal one."

SUMMARY

1. An organization will cope with change more successfully if it has a significant proportion of employees with personality characteristics associated with flexibility.

2. Bureaucratic structures tend to employ individuals with mechanistic and relatively inflexible personalities and equally seek to socialize their employees towards acceptance of the bureaucratic form.

3. As a result, whenever bureaucratic organizations need to change rapidly, they experience low efficiency, low productivity, high labour turnover, and increased absenteeism during and after the change.

4. The problems of change management in bureaucracies are exacerbated by their centralized decision-making structure and universalistic philosophy.

5. "A successful change includes three aspects : unfreezing the present level, moving to a new level and freezing group life on the new level." (Kurt Lewin)

6. Organizations are not entirely free to choose the degree of flexibility they require; they are subject to constraints imposed by the technology, the typical form of accountability employed, size, the external environment, and a "natural" tendency to drift in a bureaucratic direction.

7. "The belief that there is 'only one best way of doing most things' is a useful predictor of the individual's *inability* to cope with change." (Denis Pym)

8. Management principles should be treated with reserve, if not downright scepticism.

9. Managers may display their resistance to change either by clinging more resolutely to old and once successful procedures, or by grasping any innovation as the answer to all their problems, much as a drowning man clings to a piece of driftwood.

CHAPTER 6

Techniques for Implementing Change*

CHANGE AND THE GROUP

From what we have learned already about equilibrium and homeostasis in both individuals and collectivities, we know that the work group exists as a balance of forces producing a norm of behaviour which reconciles the pressures both for and against high rates of output. Much the same field of forces applies to each person's dynamic state of adjustment to his job. For example, the amount of time a salesman spends in calling on customers depends on the relationship between such conflicting forces as the desire for more income as opposed to the desire for more leisure, personal satisfaction from meeting people as opposed to the onset of fatigue at the end of the day, and the desire to meet management's expectations as opposed to the disappointment of not making a sale. Out of this mixture emerges an equilibrium that remains more or less constant unless new forces appear or existing ones are altered.

We have also discovered that if management wishes to alter the existing equilibrium for some reason, it has two basic strategies which it can employ : the promise of *rewards* (like more money, greater security) if change is accepted, or the threat of *punishment* (dismissal or reduced earnings) if change is not accepted. In practice, most managements tend to operate a combination of these strategies, with the emphasis heavily on the punishment-oriented approach. But whatever techniques are adopted, it is essential to recognize that *organizational change focuses on the group, not on the individual.* It is well known that a person's behaviour is firmly rooted in the groups to which he

* The layout and much of the content of this section owes a great deal to P. Spencer and C. Sofer, "Organisational Change and its Management", *Journal of Management Studies*, Vol. 1 (1), March 1964.

belongs. It, therefore, seems plausible that the most fruitful approach for individual change would be to encourage change in the group's attitudes and norms. "Perhaps one might expect single individuals to be more pliable than groups of like-minded individuals. However, experience in leadership training, in changing of food habits, work production, criminality, alcoholism, prejudices, all seem to indicate that it is usually easier to change individuals formed into a group than to change any of them separately."[143]

Interesting support for this view was gained by the author in a recent research study involving a company's geographical relocation. Employees had to choose between moving with the company or becoming redundant, and although the choice was clearly a matter for the individual, in any given department or section the "mobility response" was either above 75 per cent or below 25 per cent, suggesting powerfully that conformity with group behaviour played a part in the ultimate decisions of individuals. The explanation of such phenomena appears to lie in the fact that people do not like to be placed in the highly uncomfortable position of role conflict* in relation to the expectations originating from his colleagues in the group. In a word, people do not enjoy being deviant.

---

* Empirical evidence for the existence of role conflict can be located in a recent study of the performance of worker directors in the British Steel Corporation. Some local directors initially resented the intrusion of the worker directors, who themselves sensed a feeling of social rejection. In several instances, it was established that industrial relations were not discussed at board meetings attended by the worker directors. The Trades Union Congress showed little interest; the worker directors felt themselves to be cut off from their own trade unions and were regarded with suspicion if they tried to attend union meetings as ordinary members. Most of the directors faced jealousy and suspicion from their former work-mates. "Workers would put away newspapers when I walked past, as if I was a gaffer," said one. Because the worker directors were appointed by management, they were suspected of being "bought off". Finally, foremen were unsure of their authority over the worker directors and middle management was openly hostile. (V. Hanna, "Worker Directors Win a Reprieve", *Sunday Times*, 5 March, 1972). Perhaps the British Steel Corporation would have benefited from the study by Emery and Thorsrud of worker directors in Norway, which shows that employee representatives on the board find it very difficult to use power in such a way that it can be harmonized with the usual corporate objectives of furthering the economic purposes of the firm and at the same time make an impact on the working life of their constituents. See F. E. Emery and E. Thorsrud, *Form and Content in Industrial Democracy*, Tavistock, 1969.

Because of these tendencies, the group is both the *medium* of change and the *target* of change. There are clear advantages, for management, in not simply encouraging employees to accept change, but also in stimulating them to participate in the initiation of change for themselves. At the same time, the success of using the group as a vehicle for organizational change will depend significantly on the strength of each member's attachment to the group. A group which is highly attractive to its members can generally exert much more influence over their behaviour than a group which is only of peripheral significance. Festinger, for example, has shown that in strongly-cohesive groups the members exhibit greater readiness to attempt to stimulate others; they are more willing to be influenced by others; and there are stronger pressures towards conformity[144]. More precisely, the greatest behavioural influence in groups tends to be exerted by those members with the highest prestige, a fact demonstrated in a recent study* in which it was shown that workers' attitudes towards their foremen only changed on a large scale once the trade union branch secretary and other committee members had admitted their own changed views in public. While it must be noted that the group member with the highest prestige may not have the qualities most prized by management (just as the most prestige-carrying member of a Sunday School class may not have characteristics most resembling those of the vicar), nevertheless, on balance, management is likely to benefit from operating policies designed to increase group satisfactions for each worker.

Whatever change process is used, however, there is always the problem of deciding where change will begin. Ideally all change should begin at the top because, in theory, the organization does not resist innovations issuing from the apex of its authority structure. This is why staff specialists (such as Personnel departments and Operations Research men) strive enthusiastically to report direct to the chief executive, for they recognize that learning can only take place at the top.

---

* A. J. M. Sykes, "A Study in Changing the Attitudes and Stereotypes of Industrial Workers", *Human Relations*, Vol. 17 (2), 1964. Similar results have been obtained elsewhere, e.g., H. H. Kelley and Christine L. Woodruff, "Members' Reactions to Apparent Group Approval of a Counternorm Communication", *Journal of Abnormal and Social Psychology*, Vol. 52, 1954, 67–74; and N. Polansky, R. Lippitt and F. Redl, "An Investigation of Behavioural Contagion in Groups", *Human Relations*, Vol. 3 (4), 1950, 319–348.

Unfortunately, the power of command is not always equal to the power of resistance—by younger managers, professionals, and employees in general, who reject authoritarian management even when it is disguised as paternalism. Some individuals most anxious to innovate are themselves relatively low on the hierarchical ladder and even if technically they are on the same level as others, they may suffer some status inferiority because, say, they do not contribute directly to production and sales. This applies with particular virulence to the Personnel and Training functions, whose staff must therefore resort to devious methods in order to gain their ends. If top management cannot be persuaded to attend courses, then perhaps they can be persuaded to attend (preferably as speakers) seminars, conferences, or colloquia, where ostensibly their contribution will be more important than their own resultant attitude change. There seems little doubt that external consultants convey a credibility—and therefore an impetus for change—to top management which the Personnel Manager can rarely acquire; consequently Personnel departments are keen to engage the services of consultants, especially if it is known in advance that the particular consultant engaged is likely to recommend those changes which the Personnel Department have already decided they want. This may seem exaggerated and cynical, but it is, in my view, a recognition of the fact that the successful implementation of organizational change requires behaviour to be manipulated (and "manipulated" is not too strong a word) not only among subordinates but also among super-ordinates.

THE USE OF PILOT PROJECTS

According to this technique, the initiators of a proposed change undertake to make specific (and agreed) alterations to the existing organization on an experimental basis. After a given period of time, an attempt is then made to analyse the change in terms of "before" and "after" criteria on the implicit understanding that if the change has been "unsuccessful", it will be withdrawn. The principal advantages of this tactic are as follows.[145]

It helps to solve the practical difficulties of change not foreseen in the preliminary planning. For example, W. Douglas Seymour[146] has described the problems encountered by Wilmot Breeden in introducing new methods of manufacturing door locks for cars in an attempt to increase output without a corresponding increase in space or manpower. When the change was begun the company operated a day shift only, and although progress was moderately satisfactory, achievement of effective performance levels was held up by all sorts of initial teething troubles, like unforeseeable breakdowns of machinery, delays in the supply of components, and inconsistency of components. When the company had to initiate an evening shift to cope with increased orders, however, virtually none of these difficulties was met, partly because management had learned from its experiences on the day shift. In other words, the pilot project approach (although the changes at Wilmot Breeden did not, strictly speaking, come into this category) serves a useful purpose in providing management with valuable lessons on the implementation of change so that potentially embarrassing mistakes can be confined within a limited area*.

It helps to reassure the less confident members of the organization that the proposed scheme is workable. Thus arguments for the introduction of a particular change on an experimental basis are an important factor in the process of winning additional support for the change. They also serve the equally useful purpose of allaying fears about, and hostility towards, the proposed change, since there is generally little to be gained, in the long run, from presenting changes in ways which maximize conflict and tension among those involved.

Managers outside the experimental change or even directly concerned

---

* In the Wilmot Breeden case, there were other reasons why the change was more successfully introduced on the evening shift. For one thing the evening workers' favourable attitude towards the new machines were a product of the fact that the machines had by then been fully accepted by the day workers. Also, the evening shift operators voluntarily set themselves the task of equalling the productivity of the day workers, so that the situation became competitive. Possibly, too, resistance to change among the evening workers was lower because they had less of a personal "investment" in the firm or in existing methods. For the most part they were either part-time employees or were full-time workers who had been with Wilmot Breeden for a shorter period than most of the day workers. It is true that Seymour denies the existence of any resistant attitudes among the day workers, but it seems probable that this was a factor in the large spate of initial teething troubles. Whatever the precise reasons, however, it is a fact that "The rated level of production on evening shift was attained after three weeks retraining—a level not attained by the original day shift till more than six months had elapsed."

with it need not become emotionally committed at an early stage of the proceedings. Quite often a manager who initiates change becomes so closely identified with it that he cannot accept its failure until a very large sum of money has been lost or a vast amount of damage has been done. In such cases the point is easily reached where the failure of a particular change is seen in purely personal terms as an unendurable loss of prestige for the innovator. This not only means that a change is sometimes sustained long after it should have been dropped, but it also militates against change itself because people are not prepared to risk putting their heads on the chopping-block unless success is a virtual certainty. Where it is clear that the change is purely experimental, however, managers may subsequently commit themselves, if it looks successful, or may dissociate themselves if it fails, a situation which looks remarkably like opportunism but does at least enable change to be accomplished without a major emotional crisis.

Robert Heller[147] has drawn attention to the manufacture of the Imp mass-market car by Rootes (now part of Chrysler), as a project which was continued despite the all-too-obvious fact that it was doomed to failure. "The wrong decision was compounded by building the Imp in the wrong place, Scotland, in the wrong price/size category, competing at the static and least profitable bottom end of the market, and with wrong production engineering." As Heller concludes, "Rootes never got near break-even, though its managers continued to pursue the impossible, like knights after the Holy Grail."

Sayles and Strauss[216] have admirably summarized the compensating disadvantages of the pilot project process :

(1) A tentative change may be unwise if the employees have no power to participate in making the final decision about whether to adopt the experimental practice completely or not, assuming that it has proved successful during its trials.

(2) Experimental changes only prolong the inevitable period of tension and uncertainty surrounding any change.

(3) Pilot changes generally involve a period of close (or closer than normal) supervision, which can be disruptive if carried on for a long time.

(4) There is always the chance that employees will in fact "participate" in the final decision by affecting the success or otherwise of the experimental period, through such techniques as sabotage or boycotts.

(5) Changes observed in a particular sector of the plant may not be replicated if applied to the plant as a whole*.[149]

One further consideration is that cost may limit the extent to which pilot projects may be employed in practice. It may be feasible to install a vending machine on an experimental basis, but out of the question for a computer. The duration of the experimental period has to be watched carefully, too, since it must be long enough to outlast the novelty impact of the probationary change. In general terms, virtually any change in environmental working conditions—such as the installation of piped music or rubber plants—can be associated with consequent rises in productivity, but these have a strong tendency to disappear once people become accustomed to the innovation.

A classic example of the pilot project technique (and, incidentally, an illustration of the participative approach) concerns the Harwood Manufacturing Corporation, a pyjama-producing concern of Marion, Virginia[150]. A feature of pyjama manufacturing, especially in the U.S.A., is that frequent changes in style trends necessitate alterations in

---

* This point is demonstrated excellently by the attempts to find an institutional form in the Western Electric Company which could reproduce and maintain the Hawthorne effect. The company's management decided to try to do so by instituting a programme of employee counselling, which commenced in 1936 with a team of five counsellors covering 600 employees and grew to a peak of 55 counsellors covering 21 000 employees in 1948. Thereafter the activity declined and was finally discontinued in 1956. Although the major account of this venture does not explicitly describe reasons for its failure, certain speculations can be made. The programme was expensive, not only in terms of direct costs but also in the hidden costs of employee and supervisory time. In the annual budget reviews there would be little to show in the way of measurable benefits. As the original management which had introduced the plan disappeared from the scene, enthusiasm was dissipated. My own view, moreover, is that some of the very reasons which were responsible for the successes achieved in the initial Hawthorne experiments were absent when a similar approach was tried with the whole organization. We are told, for example, that the girls in the Relay Assembly Test Room enjoyed substantially higher status among their work colleagues because of their participation in the research programme, but clearly this advantage would disappear if the experimental situation (or, in this instance, a counselling service) were created on an organization-wide basis.

pyjama designs. Such alterations imply changes in work assignments and the re-learning of tasks. These periods are usually accompanied by reduced piece-rate earnings until the operators can regain their pre-change levels. Occasionally they fail to attain these levels at all. For these reasons, therefore, there is considerable resistance to design changes.

On the occasion of the study, the company saw the need for job changes as an opportunity for an experiment in the possible advantages of participation. Four groups of sewing-machine operators were formed, all four groups being matched for the difficulty of their new tasks, for the amount of change in their jobs, and for their productivity levels prior to the experiment. They were then treated in three different ways. A *control group* underwent the change according to normal factory procedure, whereby the group members were given an explanation of why a change in job methods was necessary, what the new tasks would be like, and what the new piece rates would be. With *experimental group 1*, a moderate degree of participation was employed. The members received more information and explanation about the need for change, and were invited to choose representatives who, in turn, participated in designing the new job, setting the new piece rate, and later in training the remaining members of the group. The feeling of participation achieved was such that group members spoke of the new job and the new piece rates as "our job" and "our piece rate". Carrying the process a stage further, *experimental groups 2 and 3* participated directly in designing the new jobs and setting the new piece rates.

In the event, not only was the change in productivity after the work alterations proportional to the degree of participation of the three groups, but turnover rates and amounts of aggression expressed against management were inversely proportional to the degree of participation. Immediately after the work changes, the control group's output dropped (this was the usual consequence of such changes within the company) and never recovered. Many of its members left the firm altogether. Experimental group 1 suffered an initial reduction in output, but recovered over time and finally reached a norm only just below that achieved by experimental groups 2 and 3, whose productivity scarcely fell at all throughout the change period. Indeed, these latter groups soon achieved an output norm well above that employed in the pre-change situation. While it may be true that the adverse performance of the control group was somewhat larger than usual (because its members were no doubt aware of the far more favourable treatment being accorded to the other three groups in the same organization), this study nevertheless demonstrates the potential value of the pilot project approach to the initiation of change.

Although not intended as such, the organizational changes completed in British European Airways between 1962 and 1971* deserve to be classified in the pilot project category principally because "Stage 2" of the reorganization was dependent on the experience gained in "Stage 2". Although the weaknesses of B.E.A.'s organization structure first became apparent in 1962, no immediate managerial action followed. By 1964, E. J. Miller and A. K. Rice from the Tavistock Institute were examining the problem. Still no action took place until November 1967, when some of the functions of the Traffic department were merged with the Commercial and Sales department. Simultaneously, Flight Operations, Cabin Services and London Ground Operations were grouped into an Operations division. The intention was to create a number of virtually independent "profit centres". Thus Traffic and Sales bought aircraft capacity from Operations, which in turn bought maintenance from the Engineering division. The central services, such as Personnel, were allowed to charge for their services whenever it was practicable to do so without incurring excessive accounting costs.

In the subsequent three years, B.E.A. suffered several financial losses and a few other problems, not all of which could be blamed on the new structure. The profit centre idea, as applied in 1967, created serious co-ordination issues. In keeping Traffic and Sales separate from Operations, B.E.A. had destroyed the essential unity in the process of collecting passengers and dispatching them to the right places at the right time, since the former was the responsibility of Traffic and Sales, while control of the aircraft came within the purview of Operations. If an aircraft had to be taken out of service, or a bus became delayed in a traffic jam, swift concerted action to minimize inconvenience to

---

* This case also demonstrates the difficulties attached to the concept of change in a bureaucracy. It is arguable that, in practice, B.E.A. took no initiatives in implementing change until the last possible moment, by which time the degree of change required was tantamount to a crisis.

passengers was difficult, particularly in matters like baggage handling. These anomalies were removed in "Stage 2" of the reorganization, implemented in April 1971. Principally, traffic and operational functions were brought together into a new Operations division, while B.E.A.'s regional managers were to report to a "Mainline" division controlling most of the scheduled passenger services. This was clearly a far more logical approach to the problem and certainly obviated some of the worst excesses of the 1967 changes.[151]

PARTICIPATIVE MANAGEMENT

So much has been written about the value of participative management, particularly in liberal-democratic societies, that it seems worthwhile to examine the precise meaning of participation in some detail. Perhaps it is easier to adopt the negative approach and to state that participation is *not* merely another useful item in the manager's "bag of managerial tricks" whereby "the idea is to handle them (the employees) so skilfully that they come up with the answer which the manager had in the first place, but believing it was their own."[152] Managers addicted to this application of the method clearly see participation merely as a manipulative device for getting people to do what they want, whereas in fact true participation implies three distinct processes* :

(1)   Analysing the problem and arriving at the best solution the manager can find;

(2)   Calling his subordinates together to discuss the problem;

(3)   Leaving the meeting with a better solution than the one the manager went in with.

This definition indicates both the meaning of participation and that confidence in subordinates which is essential for its effective use. It follows from this that genuine participation cannot be achieved on a "one-off" basis†.

* As defined by Lawrence Appley, President of the American Management Association, and quoted in D. McGregor, Ref. 152, p. 141.

† Professor Kenneth Walker, in *The Times* Management Lecture for 1970, distinguished four broad categories of participation: in ownership, government, management of the firm, and in setting the terms and conditions of employment. Although it is primarily participation in management which is being considered

Keith Davis[153] has suggested that participation must be a continuous process, initiated without regard for any particular forthcoming change, otherwise constant fluctuations in the organization (between participation and non-participation) merely create confusion and mistrust. One form of alleged participation, for example, is an interactive discussion between management and workers, giving management an opportunity to communicate and workers an opportunity to complain. If the workers simply listen politely, however, the participation-content of the dialogue is negligible*. They must feel free to raise important issues, and in this sense the volume of complaints voiced by workers is a favourable measure of the extent to which a participative atmosphere has been created.

It is also a mistake to assume that participation eliminates conflict. Douglas McGregor's own experience[154] is revealing : "Unconsciously, I suspect, I hoped to duck the unpleasant necessity of making difficult decisions, of taking responsibility for one course of action among many

---

here, it should be noted that participation does take these other forms, in companies like I.C.I. (through job enrichment), Avon Rubber (payment systems) and Firestone (discipline). Globerson argues more widely that a participative situation exists "where employees are involved in the life of the enterprise above and beyond their direct job duties." Thus the mere sharing of information by management, or operation of a suggestions scheme, exhibit a degree of participation. See A. Globerson, "Spheres and Levels of Employee Participation in Organizations", *British Journal of Industrial Relations*, Vol. 8 (2), July 1970, 252–262.

* It has been recognized, for example, that attempts to formalize consultative processes at Kalamazoo Limited, the business equipment firm based in Birmingham, failed principally on these grounds. In the words of the company's Personnel Director, "If you want to talk more about the state of the lavatories, you must be prepared to provide advance information about trading." Yet in other respects Kalamazoo is a model of participation, at least in co-partnership, since effective ownership of the firm has passed to the employees through the Kalamazoo Workers' Alliance, set up in 1948 and owning 51 per cent of the company's equity. (D. Thomas, "The Clue to Kalamazoo", *Management Today*, December 1971, 85–89, 122, 126.) As Lupton comments, "A response from management which seeks skilfully to manipulate behaviour *via* participative procedures, consultative machinery, good communications, etc., and, in doing so, offers the shadow of involvement rather than the substance, leaving the real control very much where it is already, will not for long be acceptable." See T. Lupton, "Organisational Change : 'Top-Down' or 'Bottom-Up' Management?", *Personnel Review*, Vol. 1 (1), Autumn 1971, 22–28.

uncertain alternatives, of making mistakes and taking the consequences. I thought that maybe I could operate so that everyone would like me —that 'good human relations' would eliminate all discord and disappointment. I could not have been more wrong."

In practice, as a recent article[155] on the subject has indicated, there are three reasons for using participative methods, and none of them concerns the manager's desire to avoid his responsibilities as boss. First, the use of consultative methods does not imply that a consensus is obligatory, since the final decision must be made by the manager himself. Secondly, participation implies that subordinates are given the reasons for management decisions and are informed of future plans. Thirdly, if the manager is to reap the benefits of participation, he must truly represent "the group to the outside world, and the outside world to the group". In sum, autocracy gives "decisive action, speed, drive and, because of discipline, predictable behaviour once a decision is made." Participation, on the other hand, produces "individual satisfactions, wiser decisions (because the ideas of others have been incorporated), commitment to the decision because the group has shared in it, and some development of individuality in management decision-making". Either way, however, the ultimate criterion of management performance is the attainment of results, whatever approach is used. "Thus, a well-known London company a few years ago was widely reputed to be an ideal firm to work for because of its splendid personnel policies, canteen and sports facilities and because of the worker involvement and job satisfaction on every hand. But it forgot to satisfy its customers and went out of business."

Current theories on the effectiveness of participation owe much to the experimental evidence collected by Kurt Lewin and others during the last war. One such study concerned the attempt to persuade American housewives to cook offal*. Three approaches were used: lecture-demonstrations, doorstep interviews and discussion groups, the latter being composed of about 13 to 17 housewives. The discussions dealt with such subjects as the problems of changing eating habits in wartime, the relative importance of diet, smell and flavour, and other related topics. Only after the discussions were well launched and the

---

* This account is adapted from M. Ivens and F. Broadway, eds., *Case Studies in Management*, Business Publications, 1964, 254.

housewives were thoroughly interested in the problems did the demonstrator come forward with some useful tips on how to solve them. Follow-up studies showed that of the housewives who attended the lectures (essentially one-way communication), three per cent subsequently served offal, compared with 32 per cent of those participating in the discussion groups. The members of the latter also persevered with the new meats for longer periods than the other two groups. Summing up the general implications, Cartwright and Zander[156] point out that "Group decisions have been shown to be more effective than other methods in stimulating changes of behaviour, such as : feeding babies orange juice; increasing production of pyjamas; improving reliability of merit ratings; examining breasts for cancer; serving brains, liver and kidneys; or eating whole wheat bread."

In case much of this evidence seems irrelevant to the industrial environment, it is relevant to recall the remarkable experiments by Bavelas with a number of women performing a sewing operation on a group incentive basis[157]. Having chosen a superior group with an average output of approximately 74 units per hour (within a range 70–78), Bavelas asked them to set their own production goals. After considerable discussion they agreed unanimously on a target of 84 units hourly, which they exceeded within five days. A goal of 95 units per hour, set at a later meeting, could not be met consistently. Eventually the target was reduced to the relatively permanent level of 90 units. During the next several months, the group's output averaged approximately 87 units (within a range 80–93). The net increase, after participative methods were introduced, was approximately 13 units hourly*.

The principal reasons for the success of participative methods appear to include, first, the fact that explaining the need for change to everyone involved helps to alleviate their natural fears. Secondly, the participation of key personnel in contributing to the proposed change helps to create a degree of internal commitment to the change, a reduction of the Us/Them conflict. Thirdly, consultation helps management to perceive more accurately the attitudes, values, and perceptions of their

* This experiment has subsequently been repeated with similar results; see L. C. Lawrence and P. C. Smith, "Group Decision and Employee Participation", *Journal of Applied Psychology*, Vol. 39, October 1955, 334–337.

subordinates so that future changes can be planned in ways that minimize conflict. It is also widely believed that job satisfaction is enhanced when an employee has the opportunity to participate in decisions affecting his work, although the evidence here is ambiguous*. Finally, consultation may even be a positive source of motivation towards change in the future, in that it spreads a general awareness of the need for change, provides a better understanding of what is entailed, and brings employees closer to the intricacies and difficulties of actual planning. In a recent article on office landscaping (Burolandschaft), for example, it is suggested that the ideal method of implementing the changes involved is the creation of a planning team made up of management, systems analysis, architects, and staff representatives, in the hope that the employee co-operation essential to the success of the project can thus be guaranteed[158]. Whether this is true in any particular case or not, it certainly seems likely that the success of any such change introduced *without* some measure of consultation would be problematical.

Clearly, if participative methods are to be employed, the change cannot be pre-planned in precise detail. The process demands a good deal of flexibility, with constant reviews and consultations as progress is made. If targets are set, it is desirable that they should take the form of relatively simple sub-goals rather than an overall objective in global terms, either because the overall objective may itself alter as the participative process proceeds, or because the overall objective has already been set elsewhere. In contemplating the introduction of a three-shift system, for instance, the company may take the major policy decision but may leave it to the workers themselves to determine what form the shifts and the rota system will take.

The practical implementation of participative management, together with the severe problems, has been discussed in a case-study of ex-

---

* A recent study among elected members of workers' councils in Yugoslavia, for example, concluded that the experience of participation had no effect upon job satisfaction. Indeed, the council members, characterized by a higher level of aspiration than their non-participating colleagues, seemed to suffer from higher levels of frustration because the reality of relationships within the workers' councils did not allow them to exercise as much power as they would like. See J. Obradovic, J. French and W. Rodgers, *Human Relations*, Vol. 23 (5), 459, 1970.

periences in Shell U.K. Ltd.[159] Faced with difficulties of inadequate
motivation and low productivity, the company set up an Employee
Relations Planning Unit (E.R.P.) to study the question in depth and
produce some long-term solutions. The Unit began work in 1964 and
published its findings a year later. Two major problem areas were
identified : first, the unfavourable or negative attitudes which many
hourly-paid employees had towards their jobs and towards the company; and secondly, the many restrictive terms and conditions of
employment which had been incorporated over the years in trade union
agreements. It was suggested that these two problems were linked. Until
a more favourable organizational climate and more positive attitudes
could be induced, there were limits to what could be achieved through
conventional productivity bargaining. "Fundamentally the men are not
committed to the company's objective and the most we can hope for is
that they will honour the bargain they have entered into."*

The E.R.P. report then recommended a long-term policy to secure
a fundamental change in attitude on the part of employees†.

Such a change could only be achieved if the attitudes at all levels of
supervision and management were altered in the same direction, namely,
towards increased participation in objective-setting and increased feedback in communication systems. On the mechanics of attitude change,

* Experience at the Esso refinery, Fawley, had shown that while the men
were prepared to fulfil the terms of their agreements with management, they
were not prepared to extend their co-operation to cover any work not specifically
mentioned in the agreements. See A. Flanders, *The Fawley Productivity Agreements*, Faber and Faber, 1964.

† The idea that low productivity is basically attributable to negative attitudes
is, of course, not new. A large number of productivity teams visiting the U.S.A.
after World War II had come to the same conclusion. In 1967, I.C.I. sent six
groups of employees to America "to study the various factors, other than technical
know-how, which affect productivity in the firms to be visited in Canada and
the United States." The groups found empirical evidence that these firms were
more efficient in their use of labour than I.C.I., sometimes by as much as 50 per
cent. The difference was not a matter of harder work. Nor were tools, labour-
saving equipment, or capital equipment, in general, very different. But there
were far fewer supervisors and managers—in both process and maintenance areas
—and fewer operatives in most of the plants. "This general saving in the number
of people employed resulted from the successful delegation of responsibility, from
the acceptance of greater responsibility by workers, from the flexibility in allocat-
ing work between different grades, from a sense of involvement with the fortunes
of the company and from a general desire for self-improvement at all levels."
See W. M. Clarke, *The Director*, March 1967.

the E.R.P. team indicated that it would produce a draft statement of objectives and management philosophy which would then serve as a focal point for discussion and debate throughout the organization. It was suggested that, in the long term, such a dissemination process would bring about the desired change in attitudes at shop-floor level. Production of the draft statement and handling of the group discussions were assisted by the Tavistock Institute of Human Relations. The result was a wide measure of support at all levels for the ideas and values embodied in the statement, and the creation of a climate in which changes in job design and in working methods could be introduced (experimentally or otherwise) with the active participation of all concerned.

Chris Argyris has described a similar participative technique for introducing change in the organization by the use of *task groups*[160]. It seems worthwhile to discuss this method in some detail since it raises some further general considerations about participation. In *Phase 1*, task groups were formed to diagnose the effectiveness of the existing organization in non-specific terms. These groups were made up of people from various management functions at about the same hierarchical level. They met twice for several hours each. At this stage the groups were not asked to define solutions for an organizational problem which emerged, because there was a danger that groups and individuals might become too attached to their particular suggestions. It was further felt that people tend to be hesitant about mentioning problems if they are asked for solutions and cannot think of any.

For *Phase 2*, the results of the diagnostic sessions were fed to a top-level steering committee containing representatives from all managerial levels. An integrated picture finally emerged, despite obvious gaps and inconsistencies, and the committee was able to compile lists of major questions to be answered before the overall diagnosis could be accepted as valid. These questions were submitted to small task groups composed of individuals with some expertise relevant to the particular topic under consideration. The groups were disbanded as soon as their questions had been answered.

Phase 3 consisted of the development of a proposed new organization structure by the steering committee. Since this necessitated suggestions for rearranging individual and group tasks, committee members, not surprisingly, began to lose their objectivity and become more involved, cautious, defensive, and protective of their vested interests. At this point the company's education Department provided a course in group behaviour for the steering committee, which helped the members to become more "open" in confronting their problems. It was at this stage, too, that the committee became more willing to co-opt members of departments whose future roles were under discussion, so that problems could be solved jointly, without overtones of authoritarianism.

The preparation of the final (but tentative) plan was initiated in *Phase 4*. At this stage the draft proposals were fully discussed with top management and with representatives of all departments. Two members of the steering committee themselves belonged to top management and had authority to approve most of the changes contemplated. As a further safeguard, *Phase 5* concerned the collection of data, principally in the form of replies to a questionnaire. From this document, circulated to all participants in the change process, came several new ideas and suggestions, mainly originating among those who feared that the earlier ideas of the task groups had been pushed through by powerful cliques. When all the outstanding amendments had been made to the plan, it was drawn up to a specific timetable and then implemented (*Phase 6*).

This sequence took 17 months to complete, but when the proposed changes were finally introduced, the resisting forces and tensions were much lower than expected (by comparison with previous experiences within the same organization). There was a high degree of internal commitment to the changes (they were described as "ours", not "theirs").

Some managers may wonder if the organization can take so much time to change its structure. Argyris suggests that "although time is a critical factor, it is a false issue". Whether management likes it or not, people will take time—to ask all the questions, to make all the politically necessary moves, to develop all the protective devices, and to create all the organizational "escape hatches" they feel are needed. If a change is introduced rapidly, with consultation limited or even non-existent, this period of adjustment is generally characterized by substantially lower productivity, higher absenteeism, increased labour turnover, tension, frustration, and conflict, all of which prevent the beneficial consequences of the change from becoming apparent until some time has elapsed. It is suggested here that drastic falls in post-change performance indices can be avoided by deliberate and meticulous pre-planning—and that this planning can be justified when its cost (in both time and money) is measured against the damage done to the organization and its members by the over-hasty and dictatorial implementation of change.

Another case of organizational change introduced effectively through participative methods concerns a medium-sized company anxious to establish comprehensive innovations in industrial relations, wage systems and efficiency[161]. In the 18-month period involved (significantly almost identical to the time taken in the experience quoted by Argyris) the company achieved, at negligible cost, a complete change of payment methods from individual and sectional piece-work to measured daywork on a variable rate. Improvements in industrial relations may be measured by the fact that there had been no wage claims for over two years since the agreement was concluded, whereas management had previously expected to negotiate on wage claims continuously through-out the year. One advantage of this was that management was left free to concentrate on more positive aspects of management, like the implementation of a structural change from a functional type of organization to a manufacturing and project arrangement. A series of critical events had demonstrated the need to reform the wage system : principally the growing disparity of earnings between jobs, and a dispute in the hot mills, whose solution was expected to generate a rash of consequential wage claims. With the consent of the trade unions, a joint committee pattern was established in order to supervise the job evaluation exercise required as a basis for more equitable payment. Understandably, the shop stewards did not commit themselves at this stage, but later they took a full part in all committee decisions. The majority obtained at the final shop-floor vote to ratify job evaluation, although just over 60 per cent, was disappointing and arose chiefly because of the lack of an effective communication structure down to shop floor level. As a result ten departmental committees were set up, providing not only a channel of communication, but also "a way of involving all the representatives of the shop floor very directly in decisions that are made." Agreement to job evaluation was only a prelude to subsequent innovations in relating pay to productivity more systematically, and although the original objectives did take 18 months to achieve, in a very real sense the impetus for change thus generated meant that change had now become a way of life rather than a threatening and hostile word.

Most experience suggests that the use of participative methods helps to minimize the "crisis" characteristics of change itself. Concerning the introduction of a more highly-automated power plant into a large industrial organization, for example, a recent study comments : "The period of transition and subsequently has not been marked by any labour stoppages, bitter disputes, deadlocked negotiations, or deterioration of management–worker relations . . . We got a consistent picture of *prior and unhurried negotiation* by representatives of all the parties concerned in the expected conflicts of interest."[162] (Author's italics.) Furthermore, if participation is employed, changes may actually be introduced *more* rapidly than otherwise. "Any problems encountered by the workers are early brought to management's attention so that adjustments can be made with a minimum of delay. The workers' suggestions can be incorporated into the new procedure before a scheme of payments is fixed. Through participation, it is possible to head off any misunderstandings that might arise. This helps to avoid any deliberate obstruction of the new system by the workers."[163]

Perhaps the final word can be given to E. C. Miller[164], writing of participation in the context of Management by Objectives. "Participation (in setting objectives or standards) tends to increase commitment; commitment tends to heighten motivation; motivation which is job-oriented tends to make managers work harder and more productively; and harder and more productive work by managers tends to enhance the company's prosperity; therefore, participation is good."

SOCIAL CONSULTANCY

This technique implies direct intervention by the behavioural scientist in the implementation of organizational change. According to the pattern set by the first work in this field, the Glacier research, the social consultant (who is responsible to the Board or to the organization as a whole) joins a number of task-oriented groups within the organization and uses his understanding—as a behavioural scientist—in the furtherance of the group task. It is important to establish that the social (or process) consultant operates by guiding the client through self-analysis to self-help, rather than by solving the organization's problems in an omniscient way. "Whereas the standard consultant is more concerned about passing on his knowledge, the process consultant is principally concerned with passing on his skills and values."[165] Another worker in the same field, Chris Argyris, uses the descriptive phrase "intervention theory", where "intervention" is defined as the process of "entering into an ongoing system of relationship, to come between or among persons, groups or objects for the purpose of helping them"[166]. The role of the interventionist is to assist an organization to become more effective in problem-solving, decision-making, and decision implementation so that, as it improves at these activities, it has less need of his help. His methods include attitude surveys, T-Groups and "confrontation" meetings in which people with conflict relationships are persuaded to talk through their differences. Argyris works principally with top management, whose problems he sees as primarily those of poor inter-personal and inter-group relationships, the force of tradition and the strength of group norms. All these contribute to ineffective problem-solving and resistance to change.

F. C. Mann[167] describes a similar method whereby suggestions for organizational change are initiated at successive levels of the organization, in collaboration with an external behavioural scientist acting in a consultancy role. At each level of the structure, once it becomes known that change is impending, managers formulate plans for fulfilling their own administrative tasks. These plans are discussed freely with subordinates, who also have an opportunity to discuss their own attitudes towards such factors as the work itself, promotion, and the degree of supervision they find acceptable. The broad aim of this process is to maintain and possibly improve morale and face-to-face relationships during a period of change (when they are likely to be threatened) and to provide all personnel with a better understanding of the problems associated with change.

A specific illustration of social consultancy in action concerns the major organizational changes which took place in the Bell Telephone Company of Pennsylvania between 1958 and 1962*, and which are

---

* The following account is compressed from K. LeCompte, "Organizational Structures in Transition", *Organization Theory in Industrial Practice*, M. Haire, editor, John Wiley, 1962.

described in some detail here in order to clarify the precise advantages of this approach. The change itself was a global project inspired by the Board's desire to cope with an increasing rate of growth, to say nothing of the need to accommodate technological changes in communications systems and the introduction of computers. Managers had to be developed to meet the demands of these changes. As a first step, therefore, specific responsibility for planning the change was given to a full-time "change agent" (the author of the article from which this summary is taken) reporting direct to the Vice-President (Personnel). Virtually his only brief was that there were no preconceived ideas regarding procedures or the end result; and no limitations were set on the lines of inquiry to be followed.

Preliminary discussions soon disclosed all sorts of conflicting opinions about the need for change, the methods to be followed, and the time-scale to be chosen. Some argued for completion within six months, whereas others said that the only way to proceed was by a carefully-planned time schedule extending over several years. Apart from getting some information about what other similar companies had done with respect to organization planning and change, the Bell change agent sought advice on these problems from an outside consultant, Professor Douglas McGregor of the Massachusetts Institute of Technology. As LeCompte says, "A widely-known independent expert in organization theory was not viewed by company people as masterminding the future of their business, but rather as a resource person to whom they might turn for help." Secondly, his advice was readily acceptable at face value, because it was known that he had no axe to grind. Thirdly, he was able, as an outsider, to work with and contact directly the top officers of the company on matters of basic policy and strategy, such as the time schedule for the proposed changes. In the event, indeed, McGregor was able to persuade the firm's senior executives to accept the idea of a more lengthy and thorough planning period than that originally proposed.

With these difficulties out of the way, two task forces were appointed with representatives of every level, department, and geographical area within the company's field of operations. While the *Planning Committee* was charged with the aim of investigating the organization and its problems, the *Controls Committee* focused its attention on the firm's current management philosophy and its management control systems.

Initially, the two committees met separately, with the change agent acting as staff and liaison. It was intended that their work should be integrated as the study neared completion.

The planning committee first held a one-week orientation meeting. From this emerged some objectives and assumptions to which the committee members were to aim :

(1) Bring the interdepartmental decision level nearer to the problem level.

(2) Keep the number of organization levels to a minimum.

(3) Re-assign departmental functions where increased effectiveness will result, regardless of historical associations.

(4) Decentralize those functions which can be performed more effectively if decentralized.

(5) Centralize those functions which can be done more effectively on an area or company basis.

The effect of these initial clarification sessions was that the Planning Committee quickly abandoned any attempt simply to redraw the organization chart. Instead, they formed sub-committees to examine specific problems in consultation with management people at all levels. This in itself took several months to complete, but from it emerged the recommendation to install a new organization structure in one area of the company's operations on a pilot basis, with the corollary that no changes would be made elsewhere until the pilot operation could be evaluated. However, the change consultant (Professor McGregor) now pointed out that a new organization structure represented only part of the problem. In fact, he said, the overall change situation presented top management with the opportunity for making basic alterations in managerial strategy, especially in the control and measurement field.

The Controls Committee, after a thorough analysis of the data and after studying the structure proposed by the Planning Committee, prepared a comprehensive report on its own assignment. Two of the suggested innovations which seem to deserve particular emphasis were :

(1) In preparing reports on the performance of district and sub-district operating units, emphasis on comparisons with other units within the company was to be minimized in favour of data on the unit's own past performance.

(2) New patterns of relationships were to be established in an attempt to give maximum self-development opportunities for managers in the new organization.

The Controls Committee report was approved. The next step was the preparation of a timetable for the proposed changes and the creation of some familiarity with the new structure. Already company employees at every level had participated in the planning process, through widespread sub-committees which in turn had conducted interviews among hundreds of people. Periodic announcements about the progress of the two task forces had been widely circulated throughout the firm by means of several special numbers of the house magazine and individual letters from the company President to everyone in the top four levels of management (such letters were very rarely issued and therefore gained maximum attention). For middle management groups, a series of one-day meetings was held to explain the background of the study and the new organizational relationships that would exist.

So far as actual implementation was concerned, the initial planning had already taken 18 months. A further six months was allocated to such matters as the appointment of new top area management and departmental heads. After activation (on 1 October 1960) it was thought that six months would be needed to iron out communication and procedural bugs, and the system would have to operate for two years before its effectiveness could be evaluated. By 1962 managerial evaluation of the pilot scheme showed that the vast majority of the stated objectives had been achieved. Responsibilities had been allocated more logically. The number of middle management positions had been reduced. Staff procedures were considered more effective. Employee morale continued high, as it had been from the beginning. It seems plausible to argue that eventual success was attributable largely to the contributions of the outside consultant (McGregor) and the internal consultant (the change agent), together with the detailed but flexible planning with strong participative elements. Certainly the case of the Bell Telephone Company is an excellent demonstration of the fact that social consultancy has practical applications as a technique of change implementation, even though there are very few behavioural scientists in this country capable of tackling the kind of task achieved by McGregor.

In an attempt to evaluate the effectiveness of social consultancy, Friedlander[168] has reported the results of an investigation into organizational training laboratories. This can be defined as a series of sessions where the purpose is to identify problems facing the work-group, to invent possible solutions to these problems, and to plan implementation. Over a two-year period 12 groups of civilians employed in a services research and development establishment were studied. Each group was composed of five–fifteen members and represented four levels in the organization hierarchy. Essentially, they were task-oriented work groups. Significant changes occurred in the behaviour of the participants, principally in such areas as team effectiveness in problem-solving, mutual influence among group members, and members' sense of personal involvement and participation in group meetings. Curiously, there was no noticeable improvement in feelings of approachability towards the group chairman, or inter-group trust and confidence.

Often the presence of the social consultant enables hidden anxieties and conflicts to be brought to the surface, and in some curious way this seems to facilitate acceptance of change. Like sensitivity training, social consultancy is basically unpleasant and painful to the individuals concerned, but undoubtedly claims greater effectiveness in changing attitudes and behaviour than the one-way communication processes typical of the classroom. Spencer and Sofer go so far as to suggest that virtually all successful methods of implementing change are necessarily painful to the participants, and that the crises which often precipitate organizational change have a "functional character" in that they force management, perhaps for the first time, to face its problems realistically[169]. Much the same point is made by Mann and Neff[170] : "A major crisis in the planning and execution of a changeover may be necessary to ensure real understanding of the change by key top personnel. Crises can assist in bringing about attitude changes in top-level personnel and should be viewed positively as well as negatively."

SOCIAL ANALYSIS*

Any plan for change and the methods of implementing it must be

---

* The title of this section and much of the content is taken from T. Lupton, "The Practical Analysis of Change in Organizations", *Journal of Management Studies*, Vol. 2 (2), May 1965, 218–227.

dovetailed to fit the particular objectives and circumstances of the organization. By measuring the present performance of the organization and then setting new realistic objectives one can arrive at a theoretical improvement in the organization's performance. It is then essential to gauge as accurately as possible the benefits and the risks involved in seeking to attain these objectives. If one could ignore the human element this would be a relatively simple problem, for premises, plant, equipment and materials can all be valued fairly accurately. Even certain "personnel" costs, such as upheaval allowances, can be fairly easily estimated. The most difficult aspect to evaluate in advance is the support that any strategy will receive from the employees. What will be the effect on morale when the announcement is made? Will there be any loss of time through strike action or go-slows? How many employees will leave the firm? Which employees will leave? Will it be possible to replace them? What kind of training programme will be necessary? How and to what extent will the change affect company–employee relations and morale? Will the company's image or its trading position with its customers be impaired or enhanced by the change?

Human behaviour in the face of change is always difficult to predict. Nevertheless, predictions must be made and provisions incorporated into the change strategy for deviations from the predicted path. It is only by predicting the risks involved that one is able to evaluate fully the merits and demerits of alternative plans and decide upon a course of action. Since it is in the field of human behaviour that the greatest uncertainty exists, it is precisely in this area that well-thought-out and carefully contrived plans are needed. The plans themselves, moreover, must include adequate contingencies to enable them to be applied to the dynamic situation that follows the announcement of the proposed change. Undoubtedly the role of the Personnel Department should be crucial in the formulation of these alternative strategies, since it is the obvious source of much accumulated knowledge about human behaviour in situations of change. The technique of social analysis, devised by Professor Lupton, offers personnel managers a well-defined framework for the proper evaluation of change strategies.

According to Lupton, the introduction of technological or organizational change involves some alteration in the field of social forces maintaining the organizational equilibrium and its replacement by a new kind of equilibrium at a later point in time. The managerial problem is twofold :

(1) How to minimize potential disturbances during the change-over period from one equilibrium to the next;
(2) How to move quickly to the new equilibrium which will give the best results in terms of productive efficiency.

Essentially, the method consists of preparing a table diagram under the following headings :

A	B	C	D	E
Strategy to be Employed	*Sub-Units, Occupational Categories and Working Groups Involved*	*Estimated Reaction (general)*	*Specific Reaction on Specific Issues*	*Crude Acceptability Score*

In column A, management should list all the alternative ways of implementing the change (ranging, perhaps, from total participation to complete authoritarianism), together with estimated time schedules. Alongside each potential "change strategy", management should indicate in column B all the organizational sub-units, occupational categories, and working groups affected or involved, however indirectly. Then in column C their likely reaction in general terms should be calculated. The next stage is the preparation of reaction estimates for particular issues, such as manning scales, wage rates, redundancy payments, redeployment and retraining, differentials, trade union demarcations, promotion prospects, and shift working, for insertion in column D. The subjective nature of much of this data makes it imperative, in my view, that the probable reactions catalogued in column D should be the agreed responses of a group of actively-concerned managers rather than representing the values of the personnel manager alone. Nevertheless it should be possible to calculate, from these judgments, a Crude Acceptability Score for each change strategy. In theory, if management actually deployed the strategy with the highest acceptability score, the new equilibrium would be reached quickly and resistance to the change would be minimal. But it may well be that the optimum strategy in these terms is not acceptable to the firm, for technological, economic or psychological reasons, especially if it clashes with the company's established organizational climate. Thus management might be compelled to choose the "next best" strategy for implementation. However, management is at least making some attempt to predict the consequences of alternative actions and the likely duration of the change-over period.

Lupton argues that in organizations contemplating change, managers actually do go through these analytical processes but largely by subjective guesswork rather than by obtaining reliable data upon which to base their generalizations and predictions. In fact, the whole success of social analysis depends on the use of the methods and techniques of investigation developed in the behavioural sciences, to ascertain *with some accuracy* (certainly a level of accuracy substantially higher than guesswork) the extent to which technological and organizational changes will affect the individual and the group. The company can choose between a variety of available techniques, such as group discussion (structured or unstructured), individual interviews, observation of behaviour, and questionnaires. Whatever approach is used, it is important to find answers to such problems as :

(1) How the individual defines his role and his relations with others.
(2) How closely the individual is identified with the group.
(3) The nature of his customary (informal) role within the group.
(4) The extent to which he is committed to the organizational objectives.

While it is true that elaborate research methods and inquiries may be inappropriate in some cases, "when major changes are contemplated it may be cheaper in the long run to use costly modern research methods as a means to predict their social consequences, than to make the wrong change."[171]

SUMMARY

1. Organizational change focuses on the group, not on the individual.

2. The pilot project, as a method of implementing change, enjoys

a major advantage in that it enables teething troubles to be solved (or the change to be stopped altogether) before too much damage is done; on the other hand it suffers from some methodological disadvantages if the participants in the pilot project decide to distort the results.

3.   True participation implies a managerial analysis of the problem, a discussion with subordinates, and the eventual adoption of a solution better than that originally produced by the manager alone.

4.   Genuine participation cannot be achieved on a one-off basis; fluctuations in managerial style between participation and non-participation merely generate confusion and mistrust.

5.   Participation will not eliminate conflict, but it does help to create a degree of commitment among the personnel involved and a reduction in the Us/Them confrontation.

6.   If participative methods are to be employed, the planning of the change must be flexible and defined in terms of relatively simple sub-goals rather than a global objective.

7.   Whether participation is used or not, organizational change takes time while people adjust and adapt.

8.   Social consultancy (or "intervention theory"), using the services of a skilled consultant, can be a useful device for improving inter-personal and inter-group relationships, especially at top management level.

9.   The presence of the social consultant often enables hidden anxieties and conflicts to be brought to the surface; though this is unpleasant, it seems to facilitate acceptance of change.

10.   Social Analysis (devised by Professor Lupton) offers a framework for the systematic evaluation of change strategies and the production of an "Acceptability Score" for alternative decisions, based on data more reliable than subjective guesswork.

CHAPTER 7

T-Groups and Sensitivity Training in Organizational Change

IN ATTEMPTING to produce an effective fusion between the manager and the organization he is to control, it is possible to use one or both of two basic approaches : either to change the organizational environment so that it fits more appropriately with the manager's established personality, or to change the manager's own behavioural inclinations so that they coincide with the organization structure already in existence. Research and everyday experience suggests that both of these alternatives are extremely difficult to follow, although the purpose of this chapter is chiefly to argue that behavioural changes are feasible within the context of a pre-existing organizational pattern.

Clearly it may be impracticable to change the environment every time the managerial position changes hands (although managerial succession causes organizational upheavals more frequently than is generally imagined). Nevertheless, this kind of "organization engineering" is advocated by Fiedler on the grounds that certain elements of the managerial situation can be altered fairly easily :

(1) *Task assignment*—one leader may be given highly structured tasks with implicit or explicit instructions telling him what to do and how to do it, whereas another leader may have tasks which are nebulous and vague at best.

(2) *Position power*—the leader may be given subordinates nearly equal to him in rank and prestige, or subordinates who are well below him in status.

(3) *Leader/Member relations*—the leader can be given subordinates very similar to him in attitudes, opinions, social background, and so on, or subordinates who differ from him in one or more of these respects; or the leader may be put in charge of a group with a tradition of conflict or a reputation for co-operation.

Fiedler goes on to argue that higher-level managers could be trained to diagnose the leadership styles of their subordinates and thence to modify their task assignments, position power, and leader/member relations, so that they become more compatible with the leader's predominant approach.

> "It is essential that we realize that poor performance in a leadership position is likely to be as much the function of the leadership situation which the organization provides as it is the function of the individual's personality structure. An alternative to discarding the poorly functioning leader is then to engineer the organizational dimensions of the leadership job . . . In view of the increasing scarcity of highly-trained executive manpower, an organizational engineering approach may well become the method of necessity as well as of choice."[172]

Clearly much of Fiedler's argument rests on the assumption that organizational change may be easier to accomplish than personality change—yet again we know that organizations and groups can very successfully resist attempts to change them, so much so that it may be far more worthwhile to tackle the problem from the individual manager's point of view. The situation is made more complex, unfortunately, by the fact that so much of what people do is influenced by the groups to which they belong. "Human beings are constantly thinking about others, and about what others are thinking about them, and what others think they are thinking about the others, and so on."[173] Not only does this mean that even dyadic groups (two people in love, for example) are immensely complex, but also that any attempt to convey this complexity to the individuals involved creates an almost impassable barrier of communication.

A further difficulty arises from the conventional gap between words and action. Most executives can talk the language of human relations, but few can put into practice some of the ideas to which they readily subscribe. One of the aims of this chapter, therefore, is to suggest that T-Groups (training-groups) and sensitivity training* can effectively reduce the gap between knowing and doing.

---

* Much the same arguments are used by exponents of T-Group derivatives such as Organic Skill Training and Coverdale Training. See *Personal and Organization Effectiveness*, R. J. Hacon, editor, McGraw-Hill, 1972.

Essentially, the T-Group consists of a small group brought together "to provide participants with an opportunity to learn more about themselves and their impact on others, and in particular to learn how to function more effectively in face-to-face situations."[174] The trainer draws attention to events in the group by occasional interventions, but otherwise retains a passive role. A good deal of the group's time is devoted to discussion of leadership and participation within the group and a comparison among the members of their feelings towards each other.

Participation in T-Group work is distinguished from other forms of human relations training by being basically unpleasant to the individuals concerned. Keith Davis has described it as "a psychological nudist colony in which people are stripped bare to their attitudes"[174] and Douglas McGregor calls it "a confusing tension-laden frustrating experience"[175]. Undoubtedly it is an intensely involving experience, comparable, according to some observers, with being present at the birth of a new society.

It is desirable, generally speaking, for the group members to be as close to being strangers to each other as possible. Equally, if the group members are all from one organization, it is essential that they should not be in a hierarchical relationship to each other, since part of the aim of T-Group method is to leave a leadership vacuum (the trainer supports this by refusing to act the conventional role of teacher or leader). In accordance with the egalitarian aims at the beginning of the group sessions, a deliberate attempt is made to minimize status differences. They are encouraged to wear casual clothes and to call each other by their first names, while the seating arrangements preferably force the participants to sit round a circular table (a formula which gives greatest opportunity for eye-to-eye contact between group members).

At this early stage, the group is characterized by complete lack of agreement over how to proceed, how to make decisions, and how to relate to each other. Their situation has been aptly summarized by Charles K. Ferguson[176]:

"There is no structure except that we are all here in this room, that nothing further will be done for us, we do not know each other, we

do not know clearly what we are supposed to do, we have no
organization, no method, not even any common ideas to begin with,
and we are committed to stay together for several days or several
weeks."

The trainer may give some explanation of the purposes of T-Group
training but after this he is likely to speak rarely. Because they wrongly
under-estimate the importance of the trainer's position and contribution,
some companies try to operate T-Group method internally, perhaps
using their own training manager as the trainer. Theoretically, this may
be acceptable, but, in practice, the successful integration of all aspects
of the experience into a meaningful whole requires a great deal of
specialized knowledge, skill, and experience. These can be learned
(principally from active participation in T-Group work itself), but more
commonly the training manager has so many responsibilities he cannot
become expert in such a highly specialized area. Furthermore, if the
trainer comes from within the organization the whole success of the
T-Group exercise may be jeopardized. In the event, therefore, most
companies go outside for professional guidance.

When the group begins to function, members generally introduce
themselves and start to discuss topics of mutual interest, although at this
stage they often seem unable to prolong the conversation on any single
topic. Part of the function of the trainer consists of pointing out to the
group that they will find it difficult to identify their goals or achieve
them simply by raising a random flow of subjects for discussion. He
encourages them to focus their attention on their behaviour in the
group, here and now, and to ask questions like "Who is behaving in
what way?" and "What feelings are being generated as a result?" People
generally find this kind of self-analysis hard to accept, particularly as
they appear to be in a dilemma. They can find no sound basis for
adopting any particular form of behaviour, and they have no guide as
to what to do when the traditional forms of behaviour prove ineffective.

"What do people do when confronted with a dilemma? Their
immediate reaction is to try out older methods of behaving with
which they are secure, or else to seek guidance from an 'expert'. In
this way, the anxiety so invariably associated with not knowing what
to do can be avoided. . . . Only when conventional or traditional ways

of dealing with a dilemma have been tried—unsuccessfully—are conditions ripe for inventive action. Now people are ready to think, to shed old notions because they have not worked, to experiment, and to explore new ways of reacting to see if they will work."[177]

This crucial period between the abandonment of the old behaviour and the invention of some new behaviour is "unfrozen" since it is the stage at which the individual's former habits, attitudes, and values have been discarded—he has been left psychologically naked. It is not surprising that this phase sometimes takes on some of the characteristics of a crisis.

As time passes, group unity develops, characterized by a high level of cohesiveness, a sense of remoteness from the outside world, a marked feeling of territorial ownership regarding the room in which the group meets, and the appearance of shared meanings to words, phrases, and jokes which have figured in the group's history. It is at this point that the real value of T-Group method becomes apparent. Individual members learn to give and receive feedback of a direct and constructive kind. The trainer should be able to point out the connection between the emergence of a "we" feeling in the group and the degree to which feedback is helpful rather than punishing. In other words, when the group begins to coalesce, remarks which in the early stages would have been interpreted as insults are seen as constructive comments. Moreover, the feedback itself becomes more detailed and positive. Diffuse value-judgments like "I think you are an aggressive upstart" are replaced by specific statements like "When you proposed that you should be chairman, I was very angry, but I said nothing because I feared the consequences." In this way, each member of the group builds up a picture of how others respond to his customary behaviour, and much of the latter period in the life of the T-Group is likely to consist of the painstaking checking of messages passing between group members. This, clearly, is essential for purposes of accurate face-to-face communication, but is rarely possible in the everyday rush of organization life, so the effect of T-Group method in this respect is to heighten the impact of interaction at the personal level.

According to McGregor[178], the presence of highly sophisticated feedback is what distinguishes T-Group method from other forms of instruction.

"Inspirational lectures, or discussion of the principles of supervision, or conferences on human relations can provide us with new words, perhaps new insights into the behaviour of others, but seldom more than new rationalizations with which to defend our own present behaviour. The intensity of our own *ego investment* in what we now know and do is great enough to warp our perceptions to fit our needs."

Normally, continues McGregor, we get very little feedback of real value concerning the impact of our behaviour on others.

"If they don't behave as we desire, it is easy to blame *their* stupidity, *their* adjustment, *their* peculiarities. Only under rather extreme conditions do our subordinates even attempt to tell us how our behaviour affects them. When our superiors sometimes make the attempt, we find it difficult to understand what they are driving at, and mostly we disagree with their perceptions of us."

In fact, of course, it is not considered polite to give frank feedback in most normal situations—what actually happens is that our behaviour is discussed by others when we are not present to learn from it.

Chris Argyris[179] quotes an example of the complex inter-personal and group factors occurring in a T-Group when the group copes with the task of selecting a leader. A recurring problem is the apparent need of members to appoint a leader or chairman; typically, this is rationalized into such statements as "Without an appointed leader a group cannot be effective" or "Without leadership there is chaos." One of the ways for this problem to be tackled is for the group members to explore the underlying assumptions expressed by those individuals who seem most enthusiastic about appointing leaders. It may become clear that these individuals want leaders because they assume that, if people are left alone, they will tend to avoid responsibility—yet this implies a general lack of confidence in people and, in particular, mistrust of the people within the T-Group. Other members may be more concerned with the question of whether to trust the appointed leader or not, and thus the ensuing discussion can illustrate the fact that the problem of trust works in both directions : superiors mistrust subordinates, and subordinates mistrust superiors.

From this, the discussion may return to leadership itself when a group member says, "Look, Mr. B over there has been trying to say something for half-an-hour, and hasn't succeeded. If we had a leader, or if he himself were made leader temporarily, then he might get his point of view across." Some may agree with these remarks, but one may point out that "If we give Mr. B authority, he will never have to develop his internal strength so that he can get his point across without power behind him." Moreover, if Mr. B is made leader himself, the group will not have to face the problem of how to create the conditions for Mr. B to express his point of view. In this way the group is forced to study the problems of group membership and of participation, as well as the requirements of effectively functioning groups.

Argyris argues that the question of trust is the central problem in any T-Group (as it is for a group of any description). If it can be solved, then the group has taken an important step in developing "authentic relationships". As the degree of mutual trust increases, furthermore, "functional leadership" tends to arise spontaneously because individuals who trust each other will be perfectly happy to delegate leadership to those who are most competent for the subject under discussion. In doing this they learn an important lesson about effective leadership, namely, that a leader's performance depends very heavily on the situation rather than on the possession of an abstract list of qualities.

An interesting variation of treatment for the implementation of feedback has recently been described by Professor Reddin[180]. According to this technique, which has gained wide acceptance in Canada, the T-Group is composed of an actual work team—boss and subordinates— who must perform a series of projects or tasks generally involving some group decision-making. Instead of allowing feedback to arise spontaneously, however, the participants are required to select one or more statements (from a list supplied) which best describe how the others in the group perform. These statements then provide the basis for a discussion of individual performance and effectiveness. The statements themselves are usually related to one of the well-known management style typologies, such as McGregor's Theory X and Theory Y. Reddin claims that the method as a whole is just as effective, and its results are more certain, than conventional T-Group work.

Clearly the basic intention of T-Group method is to change the attitudes and behaviour patterns of the group's members, despite the fact that such changes are extremely difficult to achieve by conventional methods. Lecturing to a group of supervisors, say, about the typical personality characteristics possessed by supervisors in high-productivity work groups is unlikely to change any supervisor's behaviour. The most it is likely to do is to modify the supervisor's own beliefs about how he supervises, so that he feels himself to be democratic and employee-centred even if he is not. The lecture technique fails because it implies that the supervisor should stop behaving in a certain way and adopt other modes of behaviour and, more important, it contains a concealed attack on the supervisor's present methods. T-Groups offer a way of overcoming this difficulty by providing a supportive atmosphere of trust in which individuals can, as it were, graft new types of behaviour on to their existing patterns. In other words, the T-Group situation can help the individual to evaluate, experimentally, the likely outcome of behaving in different ways in different situations.

Thus it can be claimed that T-Group technique often produces an appreciable increase in the following skills :

(1) *Sensitivity*—the ability to perceive accurately how others see oneself.
(2) *Diagnostic ability*—the skill of assessing effectively the way in which others are behaving.
(3) *Behavioural flexibility*—the skill of relating one's behaviour to the specific situation.

Among the major criticisms of T-Group method is that the process involved is a sort of disguised psychotherapy and as such it is dangerous for sessions to be conducted by non-medical men. It is undoubtedly true that cases have been known of T-Group trainees who turn out to be neurotic and cannot withstand stress (to the point where a few have nervous breakdowns). It is equally true that T-Group method has close links with psychotherapy. On the other hand, there are marked differences. In the first place psychotherapy is chiefly employed on individuals whose psychological defences have in one way or another proved inadequate to cope with everyday life, whereas T-Groups are composed of people whose defences are for the most part adequate. Moreover, it is clear that the chief difference between T-Groups and psychotherapy groups stems largely from the different sets of expectations brought to each group by its members.

It is interesting in this context to note that Alcoholics Anonymous has had great success in using the techniques of psychotherapy but without the aid of trained group therapists or psychiatrists. Indeed, the kind of therapy practised at A.A. meetings is very reminiscent of T-Group approach. For example, "The most immediately apparent fact about the dynamics of A.A. is that the A.A. group is a group without a leader."[181] In a remarkably close parallel with the supporting structured sessions of a T-Group programme, A.A. interaction is not limited to the therapy sessions themselves. A well-established A.A. member will accept responsibility for a new recruit, will visit him and spend hours talking to him to intensify the impact of the method. Yet A.A. techniques do not work with all alcoholics. The drifting rootless individual with very limited powers to form relationships of any sort, and introverts who find the meetings extremely disconcerting, either fail to change their behaviour or obtain better results through other methods (such as discussions with an individual doctor). This may help us to understand why T-Groups have their occasional failures.

Another criticism of T-Groups arises out of the claim that they enhance managerial sensitivity. From the organizational point of view, the more sensitive manager may not necessarily be more effective or more satisfied with his job, and it is even claimed that some managers who undergo T-Group training become too tender-minded to make realistic decisions, or become so busy considering the ramifications of each potential decision that they never take a decision at all. Put in this form the criticism is unanswerable without more detailed information about cases, but it seems reasonable to assume that they arise chiefly from the fact that some managers are basically too introspective to benefit from the T-Group method.

A far more fundamental objection to T-Group work is that it is unreasonable to expect a short T-Group course (of, at the most, two weeks' duration) to have any lasting effect on a man subjected to the constant pressures of organizational life. This criticism is important because, although there is little reliable evidence about the effectiveness of *any* training method, it is nevertheless fair to ask that a *new* method should at least make some attempt to show itself more effective than more conventional training techniques.

Assessing the effects of participation in T-Groups poses considerable difficulties, however, since this kind of knowledge depends on whether the aims of the T-Group method are quantifiable or not. Principally, the T-Group tries to increase the participants' awareness of the opinions and feelings of others, and to develop the ability for translating intentions into effective action—and neither of these variables is easily measured.

However, several studies show that T-Group participants do change their behaviour after their course experiences[182]. These changes have been noted by both the participants themselves and by their parent organizations, and have occurred despite the problem of *re-entry* into the parent organization. D. S. Pugh[184] has summed up this problem from the point of view of the orthodox sociologist :

"T-Group training takes an individual out of his organizational role and puts him through a process that may change his attitudes, and thus may lead him to redefine his own concept of his role. But this is the only aspect of the situation which is changed. When he returns to his job the organizational demands are the same and so are the expectations of the other members in their roles with whom he has social relationships . . . The T-Group, by affecting only the individual, attempts to affect the whole social system on too narrow a front. It is not the individual but his network of social relationships which is basic, and attempts to alter it through the individual must remain only marginally effective. Indeed there is the suspicion that if a really major change were brought about . . . this could result in *increased* tension and conflict in the 'back-home' situation."

Miles, in a study of T-Group training among school-teachers[185], has tried to define the concept of "organizational climate" in more precise terms by classifying the organizational factors that could influence on-the-job behavioural changes. Specifically, he collected the following measures :

(1) *Security*—as measured by length of tenure in present job.
(2) *Power*—as measured by the number of teachers in the participants' school.
(3) *Autonomy*—as measured by the length of time between required reports to immediate superiors.

(4) *Perceived adequacy of the organization's functioning*—as measured by a Likert-type rating scale.

The individuals displaying the highest propensity to change, both during and after the T-Group training, were those with high or moderate power and security at work.

Clearly re-entry can have its anxious moments. Work associates may find it difficult to cope with a boss or a colleague who is trying to modify his usual management style, and they may find it disconcerting to have their own behaviour diagnosed so accurately—but the research data suggest that re-entry is not an insuperable problem for most T-Group participants. For example, a study by Bunker at the Harvard Business School[186] examined changes in the work behaviour of 200 former T-Group members compared with 200 others who had not attended a T-Group session. The data, collected eight–ten months after the course, was based on self-analysis by the trainee himself and the comments of six of his work associates. If both sources coincided in their descriptions of a particular change in the trainee's behaviour, this was scored as a "real" change, and Bunker claimed that significantly more "real" changes were found among the former T-Group participants than among the control group. Furthermore, most of these changes were in the following directions :

(1) Increased openness, receptivity, and tolerance of individual differences.

(2) Increased understanding and diagnostic awareness of oneself, others, and the interactive processes in groups.

(3) Increased operational skill in inter-personal relationships, suggesting increased capacity for collaboration.

A similar study in this country has been conducted by David Moscow[187] using the same follow-up method as Bunker. Each former T-Group participant and an average of seven work associates (including superiors and subordinates) were asked to respond to the question : "Could you please describe below any specific ways in which Mr. X has changed his behaviour in working with people since . . . (date of course) . . . compared to the previous year? If you have not perceived any changes in his behaviour would you please indicate this and still return the form, as it is equally important for us to have such information."

Real change scores in this study were obtained by two independent judges matching the response of two or more different informants. Moscow reported that data had been analysed for 28 senior managers from British and Irish firms who participated in T-Group seminars run by the University of Leeds, and that very similar results to those obtained by Bunker had been found, even to the point that the proportion of former T-Group members showing real changes in their behaviour, 67 per cent, was exactly the same as the proportion obtained by Bunker. In particular, the Leeds observations have shown that behaviour changes tend to cluster around three identifiable areas :

(1) *Increased openness and receptivity to new information*—such as other people's opinions and suggestions.

(2) *Increased interdependence*—T-Group members tend to encourage more collaboration in decision-making, to involve others more readily and to be less dogmatic.

(3) *Increased willingness to take risks*—a preparedness to take a stand on vital issues or to experiment with novel solutions to problems and relationships.

The Leeds research went further by trying to assess whether the T-Group experience was the main causal factor in the behavioural change. The T-Group sessions were tape-recorded; a representative sample of the recordings was analysed by two independent judges so that individual contributions to group discussion could be categorized under such headings as "Leads", "Clarifies", "Expresses own feelings", "Supports another member", and so on. When individual changes in the frequency of these categories was compared with the amount of real changes in the way the manager performed his task six months later, a high correlation was obtained between the two measures. Furthermore, at the end of the T-Group sessions the trainer was asked to judge which three participants would transfer *most* of their learning into the actual job situation, and which three participants would transfer *least*. When compared with real changes detected subsequently, these ratings were found to be accurate in 85 per cent of all cases.

A study by Boyd and Ellis[188] is particularly relevant to this discussion because it contrasted the influence of T-Groups with that of a well-established lecture-and-discussion course called "Men and Administration" run for managers in the Hydro-Electric Power Commission of Ontario. The actual method of assessing transfer of training to the job situation was similar in principle to that used by Bunker and Moscow, but Boyd and Ellis found considerable differences between the two methods in terms of their impact on the trainees. Their principal conclusion was that many more T-Group trainees showed "real" changes in their behaviour than "conventional" trainees, but that the latter group in turn showed more changes than a control group of managers who had not received any training at all. Perhaps the reason lay in the fact that "the laboratory resulted in more direct learning by experience as against conventional training which tends to a more intellectual learning about the subject."

The qualitative differences in the behavioural changes produced by the two methods were distinctive. Boyd and Ellis were impressed by the especially personal and specific characteristics of the changes experienced by the T-Group trainees. They also found that the T-Group trainees showed more variety of behaviour after their course than did those managers trained in the conventional way. "There were the quiet ones who came out of their shells to speak with greater confidence and definiteness, there were some who learned to consider more carefully before rendering a decision, while at the same time others received a spur to make up their minds. There were some with a chip on the shoulder who relaxed their defensive stance. There were those in the habit of expressing strong opinions or of holding decisions close to themselves who found that others had more to offer than they had supposed, and learned to listen, to consult or to delegate." Among the most frequently reported changes in behaviour were an increase in listening, improved contribution to, and understanding of, group situations such as meetings, and an increase in tolerance and flexibility*.

Moscow's studies at Leeds have found exactly the same pattern, as indicated in the following examples of subjective behaviour changes corroborated by the evidence of work colleagues. One T-Group partici-

* Chris Argyris has also carried out a comparative study on the relative effectiveness of the lecture versus the T-Group. The lecture groups did not increase in interpersonal competence whereas the experimental groups in nearly every case showed significant overall change in the desired direction. See C. Argyris, "Explorations in Interpersonal Competence—II", *Journal of Applied Behavioural Science*, Vol. 1 (3), 1965, 255–269.

pant, Mr. A, declared "I am less dogmatic" after the experience, and this was supported by evidence from his associates : "Mr. A is a better team man" and "He has a greater appreciation of the fact that there is more than a single specialist approach to any particular problem." Equally, Mr. B saw himself as "more aggressive on occasion", and his work colleagues estimated his behaviour changes in the same direction : "Mr. B is a better leader today than a year ago; one has the impression that he is confident, and what he does is right" and "His urbanity is more purposefully directed."

Clearly an important aspect of these changes is their degree of permanence. When does the impact of T-Group training begin to fade, if at all? In the research reported by Argyris[189], fade-out among the 20 top executives involved did begin to appear in the tenth month. However, data were obtained to suggest that these managers had not lost their capacity to behave in a more open trustful manner, but "they had to suppress some of this learning because the corporate president and the other divisional presidents, who were not participants in the laboratory, did not understand them." This again emphasizes that T-Group training is not effective and permanent unless the total organization accepts and understands the new values being adopted.

Thus it seems that the changed attitudes and skills learned from T-Group experience are not so easily erased by the organizational climate as Pugh seemed to think. Furthermore, T-Group changes tend to be retained more firmly than changes initially produced by other, more conventional training methods. Basically, there are two reasons for this.

(1) *T-Groups permit more direct learning by experience as distinct from intellectual, "secondhand" indoctrination*—in other words, the T-Group method recognizes that the findings of social psychology are more likely to be acceptable if they are rediscovered anew by each individual participant. In popular jargon, therefore, T-Group courses or seminars are referred to as "laboratories in human relations", implying that learning in the T-Group is an inductive process : the individual gains insight and behavioural skills from participation in a real situation. He behaves in his own way and can hear the responses of the other group members to his own actions (this process is part of the central T-Group concept of feedback). The one important proviso here, how-

ever, is that if the T-Group is to be successful, it must create for itself a "safe" climate in which individuals can learn and feel free to offer unrestricted feedback.

(2) *T-Groups offer their members a wide range of new adaptive responses to their everyday work*—so that participants subsequently become more versatile in their behaviour patterns. This contrasts with the narrowly prescribed formulae for "good" human relations incorporated in, say, employee-centred supervision and McGregor's Theory Y.

One could even argue (as Argyris has done) that a former T-Group member may still have learned a good deal from his experiences even if his behaviour does not change subsequently. Argyris quotes the case of an executive who was criticized by the company president for not exhibiting any behavioural changes after participating in a T-Group exercise. The executive replied, "What makes you think I feel free to change my behaviour in front of you?" This suggests that either the executive really had not learned very much, or that he had become sufficiently sensitive to realize that it would be unwise to reveal any overt changes in his behaviour when returning to the organization.

Examination of the conditions favouring optimal transfer of learning has led to T-Groups being used in many ways. One particularly promising adaptation is the use of T-Groups as part of an extensive, "custom-built" training programme within a single organization, designed to achieve several possible goals, such as some kind of organizational change, alteration of the prevailing climate and the group norms, or the insertion of a new managerial style. In certain respects, T-Group training conducted within a single company can have powerful advantages. For example, if the aim of the exercise is to implement some specific organizational change, outsiders would clearly be intruders. Furthermore, people from the same organization will provide much greater support for each other in maintaining changes which they mutually desire if the transition is to be completed with a minimal amount of disruption. On the other hand, the one-company T-Group may be inhibited because members hesitate to speak freely to a gathering which may contain their future bosses.

Nevertheless, the possibilities of T-Group method within a single organization are well illustrated by the work of Robert Blake and others in two refineries of Esso in the U.S.A. This work was unparalleled in two respects : first, in the number of managers participating, and secondly, in the major organizational changes which followed. For Esso, in fact, the T-Group experience was merely the first phase in a whole series of activities designed to facilitate a detailed re-examination of every functional aspect within the organization. As a result, there were changes, not only in the ways that the T-Group trainees subsequently performed their jobs, but also in the organization structure, budgeting and control procedures, overall refinery policy, and even some technological aspects of the refining process.

Blake's method was actually a modification of T-Group method known as the 'Managerial Grid Laboratory', in which trainees are provided with a diagnostic framework for assessing each other's behaviour. The strategy began with conventional T-Groups formed of individuals not in authority relationships with each other, followed by groups comprising intact organizational units and departments, whose role was to consider how their previous T-Group experiences (with initial strangers) had affected the ways in which they worked together. Thus the training programme as a whole was able to integrate normal T-Group learning, problems of authority relationships, and a detailed assessment of group behaviour.

The most adequate study to date involving a whole organization within a T-Group project was made in a field experiment by Morse and Reimer[191] among the supervisory personnel in four comparable divisions of a firm doing work primarily of a clerical nature. Supervisors in two of the divisions took part in T-Group training that laid stress on the importance of participative decision-making, while the supervisors from the other two divisions had a course of instruction focused on the need to co-ordinate and centralize the firm's decision-making processes. The results showed a marked increase in productivity among all four divisions, but while labour turnover showed no change in the divisions trained by T-Group methods, it suffered a sharp increase in the other two divisions. This particular study, therefore, poses once more the perennial issue of the organizational goals, or the relative importance of various measures of organizational effectiveness. The divisions advocating centralized decision-making enjoyed a *high* increase in productivity coupled with a marked *decrease* in morale, whereas the divisions trained by T-Group technique obtained a slightly lower increase in productivity without any loss of morale at all. Clearly the organization must decide for itself which of these alternatives is to be preferred.

It must not be assumed that in-company T-Group programmes are always as successful as those mentioned here. The programmes themselves may be ill-designed or badly conducted, and much of their success depends on the relevance of the programme to the particular organization's needs, as well as the degree of flexibility which characterizes particular organizations before the T-Group programme is even begun. What is at last beginning to be recognized, however, is the importance of diagnosing individually the particular training needs of the particular organization. The work of behavioural scientists has done much to dispel the myth that good management, style, and structure are unitary concepts. On the contrary, because company structures in different technological and sociological areas are quite different, one can only speak of the "right way" to manage within the context of a specific situation. Thus it is quite feasible that in some organizations training in centralized decision-making would be quite appropriate, while others would benefit from training in participative techniques. Only in this way can one explain the apparent paradox in the Morse and Reimer study, which suggested that the organization involved was apparently able to benefit from training in both directions at once. As Mangham and Cooper[192] comment, "there is little evidence to support or discount the notion that greater openness, better listening, tolerance, etc., contribute to effective company performance."*

Reactions of T-Group participants naturally vary a good deal, but they often stress the deep personal significance of the experience—particularly the implied message to the receiver of feedback that he is worthy of attention, i.e., that the other members of the group care enough about him to spend time giving him the feedback he wants. Equally, another indication of the deep significance of T-Group work may be that when participants are asked for their impressions and their evaluation of the training, they find their opinions extraordinarily difficult to express. Often, it is better to obtain views from their

---

* One minor piece of evidence is the finding by Willits that the degree to which managers communicate "openly" with their company presidents is found to correlate significantly with overall company performance. See R. D. Willits, "Company Performance and Interpersonal Relations", *Industrial Management Review*, Spring 1967, 91–109.

colleagues, superiors and subordinates about any behavioural changes that have occurred.

It seems clear that, in years to come, some form of heuristic learning by self-discovery in a group setting may eventually be seen as essential for anyone who spends his working life among groups. As yet, the full potentialities of the T-Group approach have not been worked out—in particular, the dynamics of the learning process within T-Groups are not well understood—but one of the major characteristics of those employing T-Groups in implementing organizational change is that they themselves remain open to the possibilities of continuing changes in both the nature and applications of the T-Group method.

Research into the effectiveness of the T-Group in British companies bears out the findings obtained in other countries, namely, that considerable benefits can result if T-Groups are employed in the promotion of organizational change, but that these benefits are considerably enhanced if the organizational climate is favourable to change. For example, Smith and Honour[193] found that the effect of Blake's Managerial Grid training (Phase 1) in a British company was substantially different from its impact as reported by Barnes and Greiner[194] in an American firm. Smith and Honour suggest that factors connected with size, situation, and type of industry may have predisposed the American company towards a more organic or flexible organization structure, while in the British case there was a more unchanging or "mechanistic" culture. "If this were so it would suggest that grid training had more potentiality for pushing an organization further in the direction in which it was already oriented, than for the more radical transformation that is sometimes envisaged."

SUMMARY

1.   In seeking to secure an acceptable "fit" between the manager and his organizational surroundings, it is theoretically possible to change either the manager or his environment, or both.

2.   T-Groups often produce an appreciable increase in three categories of skill : personal sensitivity, diagnostic ability, and behavioural flexibility.

3. Re-entry to the organization can entail severe problems of personal adjustment for former T-Group participants, particularly if the general organizational climate is unsympathetic.

4. The central problem in any T-Group (as in all working groups) is the question of trust.

5. T-Groups are far more effective in inducing behavioural change than more conventional methods of training—and the change tends to be relatively permanent.

6. T-Groups provide a useful vehicle for facilitating attitude change and receptivity to innovation among managers, but it seems likely that T-Groups are more effective at pushing an organization further along the road it has already begun to travel, rather than at achieving a radical transformation of interpersonal relationships.

CHAPTER 8

Managerial Succession and the Organizational Climate

IN THIS chapter consideration will be given to labour turnover (both fortuitous and deliberate) as an instrument for facilitating organizational change. However, it is clear that turnover at more senior levels in any organization often ranks as a significant change in itself, because of the repercussions set up by alterations in management style. Some attention must, therefore, be directed at the factors affecting and the impact of various management styles particularly during periods of stress within the organization.

THE REPLACEMENT OF KEY PERSONNEL

If an organizational change could be accompanied by a complete replacement of all the personnel immediately and indirectly affected, resistance to change would cease to be a significant problem, simply because the newcomers would have no pre-set standards or reference points against which to evaluate the changes. Indeed, for them no change has taken place, since they were not aware of and did not experience the organizational environment prior to the change. Yet in practice such a straightforward solution is likely to be both intolerable and impracticable, particularly if attempted on a large scale. Ginzberg and Reilley[195] suggest two reasons for this :

(1) Introducing outsiders to key posts may well have a disastrous effect on the morale of existing members of the organization.
(2) Success in implementing change depends strongly on teamwork, which is clearly threatened if the existing team is disrupted by the appearance of others with differing backgrounds.

Furthermore, it is probably fallacious to assume too readily that resistance to change is focused on particular individuals or groups, such as "middle management" or "the old guard". As A. K. Rice remarks, "Often the only solution put forward is to remove them. Faced with such a situation, many of those in charge of enterprises must know, at least intuitively, that if they rid the organization of its recalcitrant members the replacements will, if equally able, be equally difficult to work with or, if easier to work with, less able."[196] Much the same point is made by Larry Greiner[197]. In his view, the replacement of key persons "is based on the assumption that organization problems tend to reside in a few strategically located individuals, and that replacing these people will bring about sweeping and basic changes." While it may certainly achieve this end, the "sweeping and basic changes" obtained may not be quite those which the organization expected or even wanted : they may be high turnover among types of employee where high turnover can be least afforded, low morale, and constant manoeuvring for security distracting individuals from effective job performance.

Clearly dismissals are easier to arrange if they are part of a re-organization policy which involves reducing the size of, say, the administrative headquarters in a company. The changes in the Royal Dutch–Shell Group after McKinsey's investigation meant that for a three-year period from 1960 men began to be eased out by long notices and appropriate rewards. Shell's central office establishment in London and The Hague was reduced by more than a quarter, from 9000 to 6500. Although so-called natural wastage accounted for more than half of this decline, it is debatable how many would have left voluntarily had it not been for the known policy of dismissals at that time[198]. Certainly this wholesale turnover of personnel enabled the other organizational changes proposed by McKinsey to be implemented with virtually no disruption.

Whether personnel changes are deliberately employed as a weapon for facilitating the implementation of changes on a broader front or not, organizational innovation does tend to be precisely the sort of event which precipitates the transfer and replacement of key personnel. "As new problems emerge, individuals whose ways of thinking and respond-ing served the organization well in an early stage may be ill-fitted for the new tasks. Characteristically, this is not so much a matter of technical knowledge as of attitudes and habits. These shape an individual's outlook and orientation to the job, resulting in a distinctive pattern of emphasis and judgment. The more firmly set the personal pattern—a condition that may be highly desirable during creative periods of organizational development—the less adaptable is the individual."[199]

A good example of a situation where major organizational changes provoked large-scale managerial departures is Leyland's purchase of Standard–Triumph in 1960–1961. Leyland started off with the intention of not firing anybody, not even Alick Dick, then Standard–Triumph's managing director, but when Sir Henry Spurrier (Leyland's chairman) and Sir Donald (now Lord) Stokes moved into Standard–Triumph's boardroom, the clash of personalities was found to be irreconcilable and Dick resigned. Within a matter of weeks 300 senior executives (including all Standard–Triumph directors bar one) had been dismissed*. Yet another illustration concerns the drastic centralization policy and end of the divisional structure in the American Can Company that took place in 1964. These organizational changes were forced on the firm by its steadily worsening competitive position, its losses in some unremunerative divisions, and general slowness to respond to technological innovations in packaging. When the new policies were introduced, however, 40 senior executives resigned in protest. "To them anything that went against the fashionable notion of decentralization was quite unacceptable."[200] These resignations must have made it much easier to implement the centralization moves, since it eliminated the major source of potential resistance. Now purchasing, research, engineering, auditing, accounting, legal and other services (which had been duplicated) have been lumped together and standardized.

Managerial succession is itself an example of a change which can provoke intense resistance†. As Blau and Scott remark, "The methods

---

* See Rex Winsbury, "How Exports Powered Leyland", *Management Today*, June 1966, 60–65, 130, 134. Although all these dismissals cost £110,000 in compensation payments, Stokes claims that it saved the firm £1 million a year in excess expenditure.

† In these remarks on managerial succession and the subsequent references to Gouldner and Guest, I have drawn heavily on P. Spencer and C. Sofer, "Organizational Change and its Management", *Journal of Management Studies*, Vol. 1 (1), March 1964.

available to a new manager in discharging his responsibilities are dependent in part on those of his predecessor. If the latter commanded the loyalty of subordinates, the successor will find it difficult to do so and be constrained to resort to bureaucratic methods, whereas the successor to an authoritarian bureaucrat will find it advantageous to use more informal managerial practices."[201] These effects have been well documented by Alvin Gouldner[202] and Robert H. Guest[203], each describing cases where a new manager was initially instructed by his superiors to increase productivity.

THE GYPSUM MINE AND THE CAR ASSEMBLY PLANT

Gouldner's study centred round a plant owned and operated by the General Gypsum Company, with main offices at Lakeport, a city near the Great Lakes. The plant was situated 16 miles away from Lakeport at a village called Oscar Center. In 1948 when the study began it employed approximately 225 people, 75 in the mine and 150 in various surface departments. The plant's two basic operating divisions were the sub-surface mine and the surface factories. The mines worked a shift system, while most of the rest of the personnel operated a six day week.

Most of the workers lived in and around Oscar Center, which was characterized by a traditional outlook on life. Many of the employees worked in the plant simply because it was near their town. Some families had lived there for generations and over a long period of time a community spirit had grown up. As Gouldner says, "Being with their families, among their friends, living in their own home, rooted in their own neighbourhoods, are signficant values to these workers."[204] This was true not only between workers but between workers and supervisors. "Because they grew up together and have known each other for many years, the supervisors and workers developed personalized, informal relations on the job that reflect their community relations."[205]

As a result, workers came to the plant with certain expectations. One of the most prominent of their expectations was that of "leniency". The workers saw their main obligation as working or producing. Obedience to superiors was seen as a residual obligation and only thought to be necessary when there was an evident connection with the work at hand.

And in fact management did not require strict obedience from the workers to the company rules. For example, one worker stated with regard to coming in late : "They aren't very strict. You can come in late and if you have a reason, they listen to it."[206] This leniency expected by the workers and to which they had grown accustomed is defined by Gouldner as *The Indulgency Pattern*.

The Indulgency Pattern was broken with the arrival of a new plant manager called Vincent Peele. Before taking up his post he had been briefed by the executives at the main office. He was told that his predecessor, "Old Doug", had become overindulgent and that he, Peele, was expected to improve production. This was a new assignment for Peele and he was fully aware that he was on trial.

As soon as he arrived at the plant, Peele started to make changes "oriented to the efficiency-maximizing values of top management". There was a greater concern for the observation of rules as well as the introduction of new directions aimed at achieving greater control. To workers accustomed to the Indulgency Pattern, these changes were a source of bitterness. They amounted to increased restriction, closer supervision and, as a result, relationships between management and workers became increasingly strained.

For the next three years under Peele and his successor Landman, things continued to get worse until finally in 1951 the workers went on strike. This strike is described in a sequel to *Patterns of Industrial Bureaucracy* called *Wildcat Strike*[207], where it is suggested by one of the workers in 1951 that : "It's been starting the last three years", a remark designed to indicate that the beginnings of the strike could be traced back to Peele's succession.

Guest's study, by contrast, concerns a large automobile assembly plant with the pseudonym of Plant Y, employing 5000 people. Plant Y was only one unit of a total corporate organization with 40 manufacturing divisions and over 126 other plants in the U.S.A. At this particular plant, there were approximately 20 general foreman, just over 100 foremen and 2000–5000 production workers, according to the rate of production. The car assembly plant was a highly complex technical and social organization. Men and machines were organized in such a way that mass production of cars could take place. The two systems, one technical and the other social, were very much dependent on each other and any breakdown, whether mechanical or in human communication, could upset the work flow of the entire plant.

After the Korean War, the car industry was going all out to meet the demands of the market. Plant Y, as well as some of the other plants in the corporation, began to rearrange schedules and began to operate on a two shift basis. In comparison with the other plants, however, Plant Y was failing to adjust to the new demands on output. At the same time relationships between the plant manager and the workers were becoming increasingly strained. The workers felt that the manager, George Stewart, was unaware of the problems on the shop floor. He seemed to act on the principle that orders had to be obeyed whether they were thought to be relevant or not. Some of the comments of the foremen and workers were noted by Guest : "This plant is a one man show, so people are taught not to be self-reliant. Fear, that's the trouble. Nobody questions an order. . . . The trouble with the manager is that he doesn't really know what the problems are out in the shop. . . . In other plants top management starts off with an initial good opinion of the average worker. Not here. No one tries to understand the other fellow's point of view."[208]

The situation deteriorated to such an extent that in July 1953 there was an unofficial and costly walkout. This brought matters to a head. The top executives decided to replace George Stewart by George Cooley, at that time the production manager of one of the other plants. Cooley had been given a considerable amount of latitude in his previous post and had shown his ability to increase production and efficiency.

On his appointment at Plant Y, Cooley was issued with very few specific instructions from the division and corporation as to how to proceed. Right from the start Cooley set about trying to find out the reasons why the plant had failed to achieve its output target. He did this by holding regular meetings with the foremen and requesting them to tell him where things were going wrong. At the same time he went out of his way to contact workers in order to find out what their grievances were. As a result of this feedback and with cooperation of his subordinates, he inaugurated several changes as well as giving a great deal of thought to longterm planning.

Within the period 1953–1956, not only was there a substantial improvement when Plant Y's performance was measured against itself, but its performance, when compared with other similar assembly plants, went from bottom to top in most indices of achievement such as reduction of costs and labour turnover.

Both Peele and Cooley shared one thing in common. They were complete "outsiders" to their respective plant organizations and had no previous involvement with the social systems in operation there. They could, therefore, "view the plant situation in a comparative, dispassionate light", according to Gouldner. Neither had to worry about breaking any long-standing friendship ties—their only commitments were to their superiors. But the new manager of the gypsum mine faced three serious difficulties :

(1) It was a tradition that the "legitimate heir" to the manager's job had always been someone promoted from within the local organization.

(2) The previous manager had been well-known and highly respected in the close-knit community surrounding the plant.

(3) He had left behind a core of supervisors who had been intensely loyal to him in a personal sense. The new incumbent could not count on an automatic transfer of respect for the office of "manager", like that which would have occurred in a military or highly bureaucratic structure.

In the case of the new manager at Plant Y, on the other hand, it was common practice for the post of plant manager to be rotated frequently, every three to five years. This had prevented the building of any close association between the manager and the local community. Thus the new manager was not breaking a precedent that might have caused resistance from the start. Moreover, his predecessor had not left behind any staff who had been personally loyal to him. On the contrary, most of his subordinates had been glad to see him go. Thus the fact that the gypsum mine manager's arrival created powerful "institutional" hostilities—and Plant Y's manager's arrival did not—helps to explain the type of managerial style that each subsequently adopted. The gypsum mine manager tried to "overcome" resistance (rather than "reduce" it) by wielding authority, whereas the Plant Y manager saw that his predecessor's bureaucratic methods had failed and tried to meet his subordinates' demands for a more informal approach.

MANAGERIAL STYLE IN ORGANIZATIONAL CHANGE

Every individual tends to react to certain situations in a predictable way. This is equally true of the manager. There may be occasions when he is seen to react in a different way from the way other people expect him to react. But through observation over a period of time it is possible to generalize and predict how a manager will react to a given event. The way in which a manager reacts to such events is a measure of managerial style. More precisely it has been defined by McGregor as "his predictable ways of coping with the reality of the work environment."[209]

McGregor classified these into three broad categories : hard, soft, and firm but fair. Each can be seen as a means of influencing organized human effort in the work situation by the use of rewards or punishment. The first relies on punishment, the second on rewards and the third on a balance between rewards and punishment. From the résumé above of the activities of Peele and Cooley, it is clear that Peele's managerial style was hard while Cooley's was fair but firm. Although Cooley's term of office seems to have been more effective than Peele's, this is not to say that his managerial style would *always* be more effective. But in the context of the two cases which took place in the United States at roughly the same period of time, it could be generally accepted that a managerial style that was firm but fair would be more effective than one that was hard. Why did Peele then act the way he did? Why did he not use a more democratic form of management?

An answer to these questions requires a closer look at the various factors affecting managerial style in general, and that of Peele and Cooley in particular. These factors can be divided into two groups. The *intrinsic* factors are mainly concerned with the manager himself and his attitudes to people and work, while the *extrinsic* factors refer to outside influences that have an important bearing on the way the manager acts.

In trying to analyse the intrinsic factors affecting managerial style, Douglas McGregor suggested that the way managers act is determined by their orientation towards one of two sets of assumptions they have about people. He calls these two sets of assumptions Theory X and Theory Y[210]. Briefly the assumptions of Theory X are as follows :

(1) "The average human being has an inherent dislike of work and will avoid it if he can."

(2) "Because of this . . . most people must be coerced, controlled, directed, threatened with punishment to get them to put forth adequate effort toward the achievement of organizational objectives".

The assumptions of Theory Y, on the other hand, include the following :

(1) "The expenditure of physical and mental effort in work is as natural as play or rest."

(2) "External control and the threat of punishment are not the only means for bringing about effort towards organizational objectives. Man will exercise self-direction and self-control in the service of objectives to which he is committed."

(3) "The average human being learns, under proper conditions, not only to accept but to seek responsibility."

McGregor goes on to argue from these two sets of assumptions that the "strategy of management by integration of self control", based on Theory Y, "is more appropriate for intelligent adults and is more likely to be conducive to growth, learning and improved performance."[211]

It is possible to classify Peele as belonging to the Theory X school and Cooley to Theory Y. But this does not really tell us much about Peele or Cooley, quite apart from the fact that it is difficult to see how Cooley could belong exclusively to the Theory Y school.

The contribution of Blake and Mouton[212] provides a slightly more refined and sensitive tool for comparing managerial behaviour. They start with the proposition that there are two major variables affecting managerial style : "concern for production" and "concern for people". This basic concept is not in itself a new idea : Likert had conducted several studies into a wide range of industries and had already classified supervisory attitudes as being either "job centred" or "employee centred"[213]. He goes on to argue that a supervisor who was "employee centred" would be more likely to have a high-producing section than one who was more "job centred". Similarly, a manager holding McGregor's Theory X assumptions has a "concern for production" while a manager holding Theory Y assumptions probably shows a greater "concern for people".

Blake and Mouton go beyond this basic proposition to formulate a grid theory, which is an attempt to broaden the classification of managerial style and overcome the "either-or" deficiencies of the employee-centred and job-centred dichotomy. They do this by representing these two "concerns" for production and for people as co-ordinates on a graph, giving each a range of intensity from 1 to 9. In this way it is possible to chart a wide range of managerial styles in diagrammatic form, as shown in Figure 8.1.

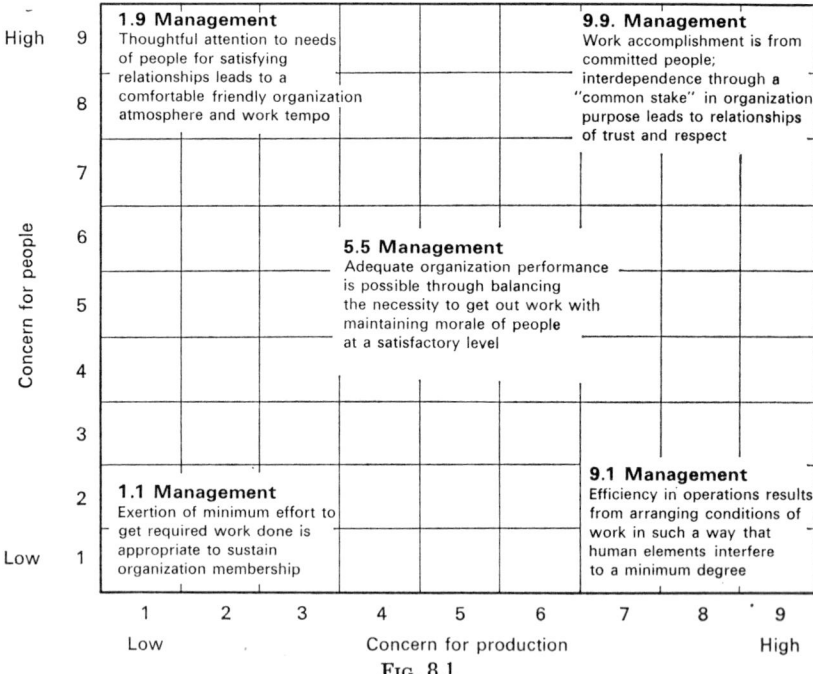

Fig. 8.1

It is not practicable to isolate an individual manager's style with the degree of mathematical precision implied by the use of nine-point scales on both vertical and horizontal dimensions, but the five predominant managerial styles, located in the main sectors of the grid, are described by Blake and Mouton in the following terms :

1.1 *Impoverished management*

Effective production is unobtainable because people are lazy, apathetic and indifferent. Sound and mature relationships are difficult to achieve, and human nature being what it is, conflict is inevitable.

1.9 *Country club management*

Production is incidental to lack of conflict and "good fellowship".

5.5 *Middle of the road*

Push for production but don't go all out, give some but not all. "Be fair but firm."

9.1 *Task management*

Men are just a commodity, just as are machines. A manager's responsibility is to plan, direct and control the work of those subordinate to him.

9.9 *Team management*

Production is from the integration of task and human requirements into a unified system of interplay towards organizational goals.

The Managerial Grid does give a wider view of managerial style. Blake and Mouton suggest that of the various approaches that can be adopted, the "Team" style of management is the best because it takes full account of the two variables, "concern for production" and "concern for people".

Cooley, perhaps, could be seen as an illustration of the "Team" style of management because he was able to achieve a balance between "concern for production" and "concern for people". Peele is closer to the "Task" style of management in that he was primarily oriented to achieving production and tended to treat men as a commodity. They were there to accept and to do what they were told.

Although an advance on Theory X and Theory Y, Blake and Mouton's analysis is still a distorted and over-simplified model of reality. Professor W. J. Reddin[214] has drawn attention to the fact that "while a manager may hold Theory Y assumptions he may be more effective if he operates in an X style. Pure X or Pure Y are less likely to be effective than a combination of styles resulting from X and Y assumptions and actions."[215] Reddin criticizes both McGregor and Blake for failing to take into account managerial effectiveness in constructing their models. Reddin's own theory certainly incorporates the ideas of McGregor and Blake but adds on a third plane concerned with Effectiveness, or Ineffectiveness. In other words, Reddin defines three variables as the essential components of managerial style.

(1) *Task orientation*—The quality of wanting to get a job done.
(2) *Relationship orientation*—The quality of being interested primarily in people.
(3) *Effectiveness*—The ability to obtain high productivity.

These three variables are related in cubical form and the eight corners

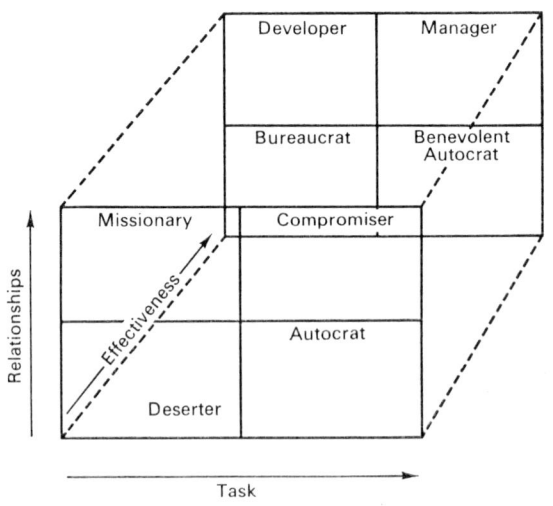

Fig. 8.2

of the cube represent different combinations of these three variables, as illustrated in Figure 8.2.

The eight stereotypes are then described by Reddin in the following way :

(1) *The Deserter* (a minimum of all three characteristics) : He shows a lack of interest in both Task and Relationships and is ineffective as a manager.

(2) *The Bureaucrat* (low on Task and Relationship Orientations but high on Effectiveness) : While fairly effective in following the rules, the bureaucrat produces few ideas, does not push for production and does a poor job developing his subordinates.

(3) *The Missionary* (low on Task Orientation and Effectiveness but high on Relationship Orientation) : The Missionary's resolute avoidance of conflict leads to poor management and low output.

(4) *The Developer* (low on Task Orientation, but high on Relationships Orientation and Effectiveness) : The Developer sees his job as primarily concerned with developing the talents of others. In most organizations he has very low visibility.

(5) *The Autocrat* (low on Relationships Orientation and Effectiveness but high on Task Orientation) : Although he puts the immediate task above all other considerations, the Autocrat is ineffective in that he makes it obvious that he has no concern for relationships and has little confidence in other people.

(6) *The Benevolent Autocrat* (low in Relationships Orientation, but high on Task Orientation and Effectiveness) : He is concerned about, and effective in, obtaining production. His weakness is that while his production is high, he is not sure how to get the most out of people.

(7) *The Compromiser* (Low on Effectiveness, but high on both Task and Relationships Orientation) : The Compromiser is incapable of integrating his ideas regarding the importance of being oriented towards both Task and Relationships. He never does anything well.

(8) *The Manager* (high on all three characteristics) : The Manager is the fully effective executive. He sees his job as getting the best out of others. He sets high standards for production and performance.

Cooley most nearly represents the ideal, in that he was high on Task orientation, Relationship orientation and Effectiveness, thus conforming to Reddin's definition of the manager. Peele was primarily oriented to getting the job done but was unable to obtain high productivity and was not really interested in people, thereby approaching Reddin's definition of an Autocrat.

The main criticism of these three theories of managerial styles is that they overemphasize the intrinsic factors affecting the way a manager acts. It is assumed that a manager's attitudes are, in fact, always constant. But this need not be the case. McGregor, Blake, and Reddin have failed to take adequate account of various extrinsic factors which may conflict with intrinsic considerations. A manager, for example, may have attitudes which would lead him to adopt a managerial style consistent with Theory Y attitudes to people and production. But this does not take into account various extrinsic factors which will have the effect of modifying the managerial style he would *like* to adopt. Sometimes the manager may either ignore or overcome these extrinsic factors and manage in accordance with his general attitudes to people and production. But in most cases the manager is constrained to modify his preferred style by a series of extrinsic influences whose importance requires some analysis.

One important extrinsic factor affecting managerial style, for example, is the social system that the manager encounters. He may wish to impose his own managerial style on a situation, but unless he makes allowances for the existing social system he may find that, not only is he unable to impose the managerial style he would like to adopt but he is unable to manage at all. Peele certainly failed to take into account the social system within the gypsum mine. His minimal concern for people was in contrast to the situation to be found previously in the mine, where according to one mechanic : "The bosses associate with the men. They will drink with them at the saloon or restaurant and there is a fine sentiment."[216]

Peele, however, was far more impersonal in his attitude to the workers and made no attempt to win them over. As a result suspicion and mistrust began to arise. As one labourer said : "He's always checking on the men and standing over them. As long as production was going out, Doug (the previous manager) didn't stand over them. Peele is always around as though he doesn't have faith in the men."[217] Peele clearly believed he could manage in a certain style, that is, one where it was unnecessary to take into account the system of social relationships in the mine. This, however, was a crucial extrinsic factor which should have played an important part in determining Peele's managerial style.

In a sense Cooley's task was made easier than Peele's initially because he became manager of a plant in a large metropolitan area. As a result no close association between managers and the local community had developed. In addition, his appointment was in line with the company's policy of appointing a new manager almost always from other plants in the division. Although there was no need for Cooley to go out of his way to establish friendly or informal relations with the workers in an attempt to win their confidence, he realized that relationships between management and workers were at a low ebb. So, from the start he went out of his way to enlist their co-operation in suggesting changes. Regular meetings were held between employees and management to thrash out problems relating to production and to working conditions.

A further extrinsic factor is the demands made on a manager by his superiors. In Peele's case, he was told specifically by the main office executives "to get production up"[218], while Cooley on his succession was given more general instructions to "straighten the situation out" at Plant Y[219]. Guest, in comparing the mandates given to Peele and to Cooley observed that : "Peele was under constant pressure, or so he perceived it, by his superiors to institute bureaucratic routines and to use disciplinary measures to gain efficiencies."[220]

It is certainly true that Peele was far more concerned with the demands of higher management than Cooley. This can be coupled with the fact that Peele was on trial, whereas Cooley had already proved himself in higher management's eyes. As a result, Peele was far more anxious to meet higher management's demands. This is borne out by Gouldner's comment that "Comments about Peele's anxiety were made by many main office personnel, as well as by people in the plant who spoke repeatedly of his nervousness. In turn, this anxiety spurred Peele to perform his new role according to main office expectations."[221]

This tendency for a manager to display the same managerial style as his superiors has been well documented by Edwin Fleishman's study of the styles of leadership shown in the International Harvester Company[222]. Several foremen from the company attended a two week course on human relations designed to improve their managerial skills. Before attending the course the foremen completed a questionnaire which measured two independent styles of leadership :

(1) *Consideration*—friendship, mutual trust and warmth between the leader and group.

(2) *Initiating Structure*—concern for getting the job done.

As expected, after completing the course, the foremen showed an increase in "Consideration" and a decrease in "Initiating Structure". However, the foremen who returned to work under managers who were themselves high on "Initiating Structure" were soon found to display the same leadership style as their managers. Their "Consideration" scores actually deteriorated to a level below that achieved *before* the course took place.

Peele's managerial style was moulded on the "Initiating Structure" emphasis of his superiors and was further reinforced when his superiors also informed him that his predecessor, old Doug, had grown over-indulgent with his advancing years. Cooley, however, did not base his managerial style on his own superiors' value system. He refused to carry out the advice of his superiors to the effect that the best thing he could do was to "clear out the dead wood"[223]. Certainly his managerial style was affected by the need to achieve results but not to the same extent as Peele.

Why was Peele unsuccessful and Cooley successful in the managerial style that they adopted? The reason why Cooley was successful can be related to the way in which he managed to achieve a *balance* between the extrinsic factors affecting the way he acted. He was able to accommodate the demands of his superiors and the expectations of his subordinates. Peele, on the other hand, felt he had to "perform his new role according to main office expectations", and this led him to adopt autocratic methods of management. In *Wildcat Strike* Gouldner defines the situation that arose as "a persisting tendency for people to seek the approval of those 'above' them. In consequence, each attended less to their subordinates' expectations than to their superiors."[224]

One further extrinsic element with an important bearing on managerial style is the effect the manager's predecessor can have on the way in which the successor manages. Gouldner makes this point in *Wildcat Strike* : "In analysing a succession, attention should be given to the 'predecessor', the man who formerly held the position, because reactions to the successor will be much influenced by what was thought of the predecessor. This is particularly true if a stable social situation had existed between the predecessor and his subordinates, so that he was well liked."[225]

When Peele succeeded to his job as plant manager he was in a very difficult situation because his predecessor, Old Doug, had been well liked and a stable situation had existed in the plant. The workers were in favour of preserving this stable social situation and in particular they wanted to retain the Indulgency Pattern they had come to expect under Old Doug. Yet Peele had to bring about change and so disrupt the existing stable social situation. His predicament was very real. However, he set about trying to bring about change in the wrong way. Before trying to effect any change it is important to try and gain the consent of those upon whom change is being imposed. This might have been difficult to achieve for Peele especially since the workers had such a high esteem for Old Doug, but he never made any real attempt to gain their confidence. Many of the old lieutenants who had served under Old Doug were replaced by men loyal to Peele. Although these factors had the effect of easing Peele's personal anxieties, they only served to increase the workers' hostility towards Peele. So a vicious spiral began; every action taken by Peele without the consent of the workers was met by a reaction from the workers.

In contrast, Cooley's predecessor had been disliked intensely. Some indication of this is seen by the high turnover rate when Stewart was plant manager and by the fact that, according to Guest, "Expressed feelings about the manager's (Stewart's) actions were almost entirely negative on the part of the respondents."[226] It would seem likely in a situation like this that any change Cooley might wish to make would have a far greater chance of acceptance than if he had taken over from a manager who previously had the confidence of the workers. As Spencer and Sofer point out : "The successor to an authoritarian bureaucrat may be better placed to introduce effective changes to the organization; he has the initial responsiveness and cooperation of its members."[227]

It is interesting to compare the actions of Cooley with those of

Landman who took over as plant manager from Peele. Both Cooley and Landman had predecessors who had acted in an authoritarian way; both then could be said to be "better placed to introduce effective changes in the organization". Yet Landman failed to bring about any effective change whereas Cooley did. The vital factor that Landman failed to take into account was that no matter how well placed he was to introduce effective change, this change could not be achieved unless he had the confidence and consent of the men. One of the men's remarks about Landman was indicative of this : "He wants to make things look good . . . get production up. He doesn't give a damn for any of the men. The men resent the whole set up. They don't like anything about it."[228] In short, Cooley was more effective as a manager because he realized the attitudes and co-operation of the workers were a vital extrinsic factor that had to be accounted for if he were to bring about change.

As Spencer and Sofer admit, the problem of succession to key posts is critical to the internal politics of any organization. The introduction of a new supervisor to a large restaurant* illustrates the proper handling of a "succession crisis" in this sense. Since the old supervisor had developed warm relations with her subordinates, the restaurant manager was afraid that her departure might have an adverse effect on the morale of the whole organization. Consequently, he prepared the way for her successor with great care. First, he discussed the problem of a replacement with both the old supervisor and the chef, her chief assistant. The chef proposed a candidate for the job and although this candidate had to be rejected, the reasons for the rejection were fully explained to the chef. When the new supervisor was finally selected, she was introduced to her subordinates at a general meeting. The Manager announced that the old supervisor was leaving and went on to say how much she meant to the restaurant. The old supervisor spoke with great emotion about how sorry she would be to leave her associates. Then she introduced the new supervisor, extolled her virtues, and asked her subordinates to show the new woman the same co-operation they had

---

* This case-history and the following list of factors important in achieving acceptance for the new supervisor, are extracted from L. R. Sayles and G. Strauss, *Human Behaviour in Organizations*, Prentice-Hall, 1966, 320–322; the original source of the case-history is W. F. Whyte, *Human Relations in the Restaurant Industry*, McGraw-Hill, 1948, 319–331.

given to her. Finally, the new supervisor promised to do her best to follow in her predecessor's footsteps. For the next few days the new supervisor followed the old one around, getting to know people and trying to learn the supervisor's routine and methods of dealing with people. On the old supervisor's last day, the whole kitchen staff gave her a farewell party. Although the new supervisor decided that she would eventually make certain changes in the operation, she spent her first few weeks trying to follow the supervisory pattern established by her predecessor. Only after she was fully accepted by the group did she begin to make changes.

In this particular example, the factors important in achieving acceptance for the new supervisor appear to have been as follows :

(1) *Consultation*—The manager respected the key position of the chef in the informal organization and was careful to request his opinion; although he had to reject the chef's views, he took care to explain why.

(2) *Induction*—When the old supervisor introduced her successor to all key personnel and explained the social customs of the organization to her, this did much to save the new supervisor from making disastrous social errors and to minimize the disruption caused by a change in command.

(3) *Ceremony*—The meeting at which the new supervisor was introduced, and the farewell party for the old supervisor, both served a symbolic function by formalizing the change and assisting the old supervisor to pass on some of her prestige to the new. The role of ceremony in society is vital at times of change (like birth, marriage, and death) when formalized rites and rituals are a form of protection against the fears and pains of moving from one stage of life to another. Perhaps more important in the case of the restaurant was the implied assertion that in spite of apparent change, the basic values remained the same : "The King is dead; long live the King."

(4) *Avoidance of change until acceptance is assured*—The new supervisor avoided making changes until she had developed informal social relationships with her subordinates.

(5) *Building on the past*—The supervisor made it clear that she had no intention of throwing out past practices wholesale. Anthropologists and missionaries learned long ago that it is far easier to adapt the customs operating in a community than to forbid them entirely, especially bearing in mind the latent functions which such customs characteristically perform. "The banning of head-hunting by the British authorities in New Guinea led to the beginnings of disintegration in the tribal society which had been based on this custom, but the situation returned to normal when the spearing of a wild boar was substituted for the original practice."[229]

SUMMARY

1. It is naïve to assume that the departure of key men will enable organizational change to be implemented more easily; although, in the short run, this may be true, the effects are likely to include low morale with its consequential implications for labour turnover, job security, and productivity.

2. Nonetheless, organizational innovation does tend to precipitate the transfer and/or replacement of key personnel (e.g., Standard–Triumph, American Can).

3. Managerial succession itself can provoke intense resistance, because "the methods available to a new manager in discharging his responsibilities are dependent in part on those of his predecessor." (Blau and Scott)

4. A manager's style is influenced (but not determined) by such factors as his beliefs about people, the social system in which he operates, and the demands made upon him by his superiors. His eventual success depends on developing a sensitivity to and a balance between the effects of these intrinsic and extrinsic considerations.

CHAPTER 9

Conclusions

As Judson[230] emphasizes, it is line managers who must carry the burden of accomplishing change, no matter from what source the innovation has stemmed. Furthermore, these line managers must have the full support of top management. "Senior management must understand and recognize the attitudes and needs of the lower-level managers or supervisors with regard to change and its consequences." In this process the role of the personnel manager, if we accept Lupton's thesis, is to advise on techniques of implementation and the desirability of change in behavioural terms. Bearing in mind the accumulated evidence on the problems of change summarized in the remainder of this book, what advice is the personnel manager to give?

At the most elementary level the question resolves itself into a basic choice between three alternative methods for introducing change, as defined by Alfred Willener[231] :

(1) Introduction without warning.
(2) Introduction preceded by information.
(3) Introduction with employee participation in the development of arrangements.

The available research evidence conclusively suggests that changes introduced without warning lead to strikes, restriction of output, absenteeism, and high labour turnover. On the individual level too, although the employee may outwardly adjust himself to the changes, he pays a terrible price through increased illness in the form of ulcers, heart attacks, and psychosomatic disturbances of various kinds. A recent edition of the *London Medical News Tribune*[232] indicated that 36 million working days were lost in Britain during 1971 as a result of

153

stress. The journal went on to point out that "Much of this can be laid at the door of management for their lack of consultation and communication. . . . There is a correlation between the level of morale of employees and the quality of concern of senior management for employees."

Mergers and acquisitions represent a particular form of organizational change likely to encourage these effects. Barmash[233] quotes a report in the *Wall Street Journal* of the "wounded list" resulting from the take-over of the Blaw Knox Company by White Consolidated. "In the months immediately following the take-over one executive developed a bleeding ulcer, another suffered a heart attack, and a third had a stroke. A fourth executive experienced back-aches, insomnia, and a sharp rise in blood pressure because of the tension surrounding the change of ownership. . . . His health did not improve until he resigned." Perhaps it is fortunate, in terms of individual health, that the rate of mergers in the United Kingdom is only about 400 per year, compared with over 6000 per year in the United States.

The fundamental justification for using the technique of *change preceded by information* is that innovations stand much less chance of being successful unless those concerned understand the reasons for their introduction. Clearly an abrupt and virtually unannounced change, like a sudden bereavement, is a far greater shock to the system, involves much more radical readjustments before equilibrium is restored, and can provoke more highly intense resistance, than a change publicized sufficiently early for the individuals involved to acclimatize themselves to its effects.

In some situations the mere supply of information to employees (which in any event is only a partial remedy for the anxieties which change provokes) is supplemented by the direct use of *participative methods*. Tannenbaum and his colleagues strongly defend the advantages of allowing both individuals and work-groups to share in the process of change, principally on the grounds that people are more likely to adjust in a positive way if they are given some control over the effects of the change upon them. This participation can be (and generally is) limited to decisions at a fairly low operational level, like the type of rota system to be worked once the policy decision to operate a three-shift routine has been made. It may, as in the case of the Bell

Telephone Company described elsewhere in this book, extend to crucial questions about the company's organization structure and whole philosophy. The superiority of participative techniques has been established both experimentally and in practice, at least in Anglo-American cultures, suggesting that as a general rule any method for implementing change which incorporates at least an element of participation is preferable to the autocratic introduction of change without prior warning. More specifically, Larry Greiner's survey of 18 studies of organizational change found that "In the successful cases, it seems fairly clear that *shared* approaches are used—i.e. authority figures seek the participation of subordinates in joint decision-making. In the less successful attempts, however, the approaches used lie closer to the extreme ends of the power distribution continuum. Thus, in five less-successful change studies, a *unilateral* approach (decree, replacement, structural) was used, while in two other studies a *delegated* approach (data discussion, T-Group) was applied. None of the less successful change studies reported the use of a shared approach."[234] These conclusions suggest that an increased emphasis on the socio-psychological factors in change should not be accompanied by a managerial abdication of power and authority, since this merely creates confusion among the participants.

The vital point is that participation nearly always helps to lower levels of conflict, stress, and tension which accompany change. "Change, particularly organizational change, can seldom be achieved without giving rise to disappointment for some of those whose jobs and prospects are affected; what is important is to avoid, as far as is possible, the resentment and bitterness that so often follow reorganization."[235] Yet, even when participative methods are used, their success may be jeopardized if they are not presented properly at the initial stage, because first impressions are crucial in determining the individual's subsequent attitude to the proposed changes.

In the ultimate analysis, the process of implementing change requires five phases of managerial action :

(1) Analysing and planning the change.
(2) Communicating about the change.
(3) Gaining acceptance of the required changes in behaviour.

(4) Making the initial transition from the status quo to the new situation.

(5) Consolidating the new conditions and continuing to follow up.

The successful completion of these five phases presupposes three kinds of skill which the manager should possess :

(1) The ability to identify and analyse the objectives of the change and those problems requiring solutions.

(2) The ingenuity to devise appropriate methods for accomplishing these objectives and solving any problems that arise.

(3) The skill of gaining acceptance and support for both the objectives and the methods from the people affected by and involved in the change.

SUMMARY

1. Line managers must accept responsibility for the management of change, although they may receive useful advice from personnel specialists on techniques of implementation.

2. The three alternative methods of introducing change are : introduction without warning, introduction preceded by information, and introduction with employee participation.

3. As a general rule, any method of implementing change which incorporates at least an element of participation is preferable to autocratic techniques, mainly because participation nearly always helps to lower the level of conflict, stress, and tension accompanying change.

4. First impressions are crucial in determining attitudes to change, so even if participative methods are to be used, they must be presented properly.

References

1. C. A. Myers, "New Frontiers for Personnel Management", *Personnel*, May–June 1964, 31–38.
2. D. E. McFarland, *Company Officers Assess the Personnel Function*, A.M.A. Research Study 79, American Management Association, 1967, 22.
3. T. Lupton, *Industrial Behavior and Personnel Management*, IPM, 1964, 55.
4. G. B. Baldwin and G. P. Schultz, "Automation : A New Dimension to Old Problems", *Proceedings of the Seventh Annual Meeting*, Industrial Relations Research Association (U.S.A.), 1955, 114–128.
5. F. C. Mann and L. K. Williams, "Observations on the Dynamics of a Change to Electronic Data-Processing Equipment", *Administrative Science Quarterly*, Vol. 5 (2), September 1960, 217–256.
6. Tom Lupton, Ref. 3, p. 18.
7. Quoted in N. Foy, "How to send Data", *Management Today*, March 1972, 103–106, 126.
8. P. Drucker, *The Age of Discontinuity*, Heinemann, 1969.
9. R. Stewart, *The Reality of Management*, Heinemann, 1963, 164.
10. G. Wood, "How to Move Small Firms", *Management Today*, January 1972, 54–57, 118–122.
11. G. Foster, "The Real European Challenge", *Management Today*, May 1972, 80–83.
12. D. Thomas, "The Freeze in Frozen Food", *Management Today*, January 1972, 45–49.
13. Rex Winsbury, "The Happenings at Vauxhall Motors", *Personnel (U.K.)*, Vol. 1 (2), January 1968, 24–27.
14. Quoted in J. Thackray, "Singer's Saving Stitch in Time", *Management Today*, June 1966, 76–81, 138.
15. J. Davis, "Lesney Picks Up the Pieces : A Cautionary Tale for Capitalists", *Observer*, 21 May 1972.
16. C. Mansell, "How to Plan Europe", *Management Today*, November 1971, 41–48.
17. J. K. Galbraith, *The New Industrial State*, Hamish Hamilton, 1967. See also Sir Leon Bagrit, "Automation : An Extension of Man", Lecture No. 5 of the 1964 Reith Lectures, *The Listener*, 10 December 1964; C. Kerr, J. T. Dunlop, F. H. Harbison, and C. A. Myers, *Industrialism and Industrial Man*, Harvard University Press, 1960.
18. D. Granick, *The Red Executive*, Doubleday, 1960.
19. B. M. Richman, *Soviet Management*, Prentice-Hall, 1965.
20. J. Child, *The Business Enterprise in Modern Industrial Society*, Collier-

Macmillan, 1969, 119. See also, J. E. Meade, "Is 'The New Industrial State' Inevitable?", *Economic Journal*, Vol. 78, June 1968, 372–392.

21. J. Thackray, "The Micro-Renaissance at Fairchild Camera", *Management Today*, May 1966, 104–107, 144.

22. Bertram M. Gross, *The Managing of Organizations*, Collier-Macmillan, 1966, 781.

23. L. E. Greiner, "Patterns of Organization Change", *Harvard Business Review*, Vol. 45 (3), May–June 1967, 119–130.

24. R. Heller, *The Naked Manager*, Barrie and Jenkins, 1972.

25. W. F. Whyte, *Money and Motivation*, Harper and Row, 1955.

26. S. Majaro, "The Organization of Change", *Management Today*, March 1972, 74–77, 130.

27. R. Jones, "The Judgment of Gellerman", *The Times*, 20 March 1972.

28. F. C. Mann and L. R. Hoffman, *Automation and the Worker*, Holt, Rinehart and Winston, 1960, 52–55.

29. F. J. Roethlisberger, *Management and Morale*, Harvard University Press, 1941, 10.

30. E. Mumford and O. Banks, *The Computer and the Clerk*, Routledge and Kegan Paul, 1967.

31. Quoted in W. H. Scott, *Office Automation*, O.E.C.D., 1965. See also, P. F. Sheldrake, "Attitudes to the Computer and its Uses", *Journal of Management Studies*, Vol. 8 (1), February 1971, 39–62.

32. P. C. Agnew and F. L. K. Hsu, "Introducing Change in a Mental Hospital", *Human Organization*, Vol. 19 (4), Winter 1961, 199.

33. Quoted in L. H. Gulick and L. Urwick, editors, *Papers on the Science of Administration*, Institute of Public Administration, New York, 1937.

34. S. Beer, "Cybernetics—A Systems Approach to Management", *Personnel Review*, Vol. 1 (2), Spring 1972, 30.

35. A. Feldman and W. Moore, *Transactions of the Fifth World Congress of Sociology*, 1962, 155.

36. Rex Winsbury, "English Sewing in America", *Management Today*, December 1966, 64–69.

37. T. Lupton, "The Practical Analysis of Change in Organizations", *Journal of Management Studies*, Vol. 2 (2), May 1965, 222–223.

38. P. Lawrence, "How to Deal with Resistance to Change", *Harvard Business Review*, Vol. 32 (3), May 1954, 49.

39. C. Argyris, "Today's Problems With Tomorrow's Organizations", *Journal of Management Studies*, Vol. 4 (1), February 1967, 53.

40. D. A. Gotting, "The Introduction of a Wage Grading and Productivity Plan in a Large Engineering Factory", *British Journal of Industrial Relations*, Vol. 9 (3), November 1971, 314–329. The plan covered a new wage payment system, a new wage structure, and new machinery for consultation and negotiation.

41. Reported by H. Willcutt and W. Kennedy, *Perceptual and Motor Skills*, Vol. 17 (3), 1964.

42. Reported by E. Schmidt, D. Castell and P. Brown, *Behaviour Research and Therapy*, Vol. 3 (1), 1965.

43. L. W. Porter and E. E. Lawler, III, "What Job Attitudes Tell About Motivation", *Harvard Business Review*, January–February 1968, 118–126.

44. A. Judson, *A Manager's Guide to Making Changes*, John Wiley, 1966.
45. N. Georgiades, *New Education*, February 1968.
46. A. K. Rice, *The Enterprise and Its Environment*, Tavistock, 1963, 276.
47. A. H. Maslow, "A Theory of Human Motivation", *Psychological Review*, Vol. 50, 1943, 370–396.
48. "Man lives by bread alone, when there is no bread." D. McGregor, *The Human Side of Enterprise*, McGraw-Hill, 1960, 36.
49. See, for example, Paras Nath Singh and R. J. Wherry, Sr., "Ranking of Job Factors by Factory Workers in India", *Personnel Psychology*, Spring 1963, 29–33.
50. W. F. Goode and I. Fowler, "Incentive Factors in a Low Morale Plant", *American Sociological Review*, Vol. 14 (5), 1949.
51. D. McGregor, Ref. 48, p. 37.
52. C. R. Walker and R. H. Guest, *The Man On The Assembly Line*, Harvard University Press, 1952.
53. C. B. Richards and H. F. Dobyns, "Topography and Culture: The Case of the Changing Cage", *Human Organization*, Vol. 16 (1), 1957.
54. F. Herzberg, B. Mausner and B. B. Snyderman, *The Motivation to Work*, Wiley, 2nd ed., 1959.
55. M. Bolle de Bal and C. Dejean, *Le Salaire à la Production*, Collection de Sociologie du Travail, Université Libre de Bruxelles, 1966.
56. J. K. Galbraith, *The New Industrial State*, Hamish Hamilton, 1967.
57. E. J. Miller and A. K. Rice, *Systems of Organization*, Tavistock, 1967, 31.
58. P. Sadler, "Sociological Aspects of Skill", *British Journal of Industrial Relations*, Vol. 8 (1), March 1970, 22–31.
59. I. C. Cannon, "Ideology and Occupational Community: A Study of Compositors", *Sociology*, Vol. 1 (2), May 1967. See also, A. J. M. Sykes, "The Cohesion of a Trade Union Workshop Organization", *Sociology*, Vol. 1 (2), May 1967.
60. S. L. Fink, J. Beak and K. Taddeo, "Organizational Crisis and Change", *Journal of Applied Behavioural Science*, Vol. 7 (1), 1971.
61. H. Kahn, *Repercussions of Redundancy*, Allen and Unwin, 1964; P. Lesley Cook, *Railway Workshops: The Problems of Contraction*, University of Cambridge, Department of Applied Economics, Occasional Paper No. 2, 1965; and P. Pocock, "Softening the Blow of Redundancy", *Personnel Management*, Vol. 4 (6), June 1972, 24–27.
62. F. Heller, *Managerial Decision-Making*, Tavistock, 1971.
63. A. Pettigrew, "Inter-Group Conflict and Role Strain", *Journal of Management Studies*, Vol. 5 (2), May 1968, 205–218.
64. E. Mumford and T. Ward, "Computer Technologists: Dilemmas of a New Role, *Journal of Management Studies*, Vol. 3 (3), October 1966, 244–255.
65. D. Pym, "Technology, Effectiveness and Predisposition towards Work-changes Among Mechanical Engineers", *Journal of Management Studies*, Vol. 3 (3), October 1966, 304–311.
66. J. Morris, "The Human Meaning of Work", unpublished paper quoted in R. Jones, "Liberating Woman and the Worker", *The Times*, 18 January 1971.

67. J. H. Goldthorpe *et al.*, *'The Affluent Worker': Industrial Behaviour and Attitudes*, Cambridge University Press, 1968.
68. W. W. Daniel, "Productivity Bargaining and Orientation to Work—A Rejoinder to Goldthorpe", *Journal of Management Studies*, Vol. 8 (3), October 1971, 329–335.
69. S. Moos, "Automation: A Worker's Balance Sheet", *New Society*, 6 August 1964, 19–20. I am indebted to this article for some of the other sources quoted in this section.
70. F. Herzberg, "One More Time: How Do You Motivate Employees?", *Harvard Business Review*, January–February 1968, 53–62.
71. E. H. Conant and M. D. Kilbridge, "Restoring Skill, Responsibility and Variety to Jobs", *Industrial and Labor Relations Review*, July 1965.
72. A. Wilkinson, "Motivating Europe's Manpower", *Management Today*, January 1972, 63–65, 126.
73. N. Seear, "Relationships at Factory Level", in B. C. Roberts, editor, *Industrial Relations: Contemporary Problems and Perspectives*, Methuen, 1962, 152.
74. G. Clack, *Industrial Relations in a British Car Factory*, University of Cambridge, Department of Economics Occasional Paper No. 9, 1967, 18.
75. For example, G. L. Palmer, "Interpreting Patterns of Labour Mobility", in E. W. Bakke, editor, *Labour Mobility and Economic Opportunity*, Wiley, 1954.
76. M. Crozier, *The Bureaucratic Phenomenon*, Tavistock, 1964, 76–77.
77. M. Crozier, Ref. 76, p. 78.
78. E. Chinoy, *Automobile Workers and the American Dream*, Doubleday, 1955.
79. National Board for Prices and Incomes, *Hours of Work, Overtime and Shiftworking*, Report No. 161, H.M.S.O., 1970.
80. H. Roff, "What Makes Managers Work?", *Management Today*, February 1968, Vol. 126, 65–67.
81. J. G. Foster, "The Causes of Loyalty Revealed", *Business*, September 1966, 41–45.
82. Enid Mumford, "The Assembly Line", *The Technologist*, Winter 1964–1965.
83. D. Pecaut, "The Worker and the Community", in A. Touraine, *et al.*, *Workers' Attitudes to Technical Change*, O.E.C.D., 1965, 119.
84. R. Katzell *et al.*, "Job Satisfaction, Job Performance and Situational Characteristics", *Journal of Applied Psychology*, Vol. 45, 1961.
85. For example, M. Crozier, Ref. 76, pp. 76–77.
86. T. Lupton, "The Practical Analysis of Change in Organizations", *Journal of Management Studies*, Vol. 2 (2), May 1965, 222–223.
87. J. Nelson-Jones, "Frustration as a Cause of Inflation", *The Times*, 15 February 1971.
88. T. Lupton, *Industrial Behaviour and Personnel Management*, I.P.M., 1964, 54.
89. D. Lockwood, "Can We Cope With Social Change?", *New Society*, 28 November 1963, 11–13.

90. E. H. Burack and P. F. Sorensen, Jr., "Manpower Development and Technological Change: Some Considerations for Revised Strategies", *Journal of Management Studies*, Vol. 8 (3), October 1971, 304–314.

91. See A. K. Rice, *The Enterprise and Its Environment*, Tavistock, 1963.

92. A. J. M. Sykes, *Sociological Review*, Vol. 13 (3), 1965, 297.

93. W. H. Scott, J. A. Banks, A. H. Halsey and T. Lupton, *Technical Change and Industrial Relations*, Liverpool University Press, 1956.

94. L. R. Sayles, *The Behaviour of Industrial Work Groups*, McGraw-Hill, 1958.

95. Ref. 94, p. 97.

96. W. H. Scott, J. A. Banks, A. H. Halsey and T. Lupton, Ref. 93, p. 252.

97. J. H. Goldthorpe, "Attitudes and Behaviour of Car Assembly Workers: A Deviant Case and a Theoretical Critique", *British Journal of Sociology*, Vol. 17 (3), 1966.

98. G. Clack, Ref. 74, p. 16.

99. G. Clack, Ref. 74, p. 15.

100. H. A. Turner, G. Clack and G. Roberts, *Labour Relations in the Motor Industry: A Study of Industrial Unrest and an International Comparison*, Allen and Unwin, 1967.

101. A. Willener, "The Worker and the Organizational System", in A. Touraine *et al.*, *Workers' Attitudes to Technical Change*, O.E.C.D., 1965, 71.

102. T. Kynaston Reeves, "Constrained and Facilitated Behaviour—A Typology of Behaviour in Economic Organizations", *British Journal of Industrial Relations*, Vol. 5 (2), July 1967, 147.

103. D. Pym, "Effective Managerial Performance in Organizational Change", *Journal of Management Studies*, Vol. 3 (1), February 1966, 81.

104. T. Lupton, "Organizational Change: 'Top-Down' or 'Bottom-Up' Management?", *Personnel Review*, Vol. 1 (1), Autumn 1971, 22–28.

105. R. K. Merton, "Bureaucratic Structure and Personality", *Social Forces*, Vol. 18, 1940, 560–568. Merton cites the famous formula "People may be unfitted by being fit to an unfit fitness."

106. M. Crozier, *The Bureaucratic Phenomenon*, Tavistock, 1964, especially pp. 195–198.

107. *Ibid.*, p. 187.

108. H. A. Kissinger, *American Foreign Policy*, Weidenfeld and Nicolson, 1969.

109. M. Crozier, Ref. 106.

110. J. Daheim, "Desorganisationsprozess in einem Burobetrieb", *Kolner Zeitzchr. f. S.u.S. ps.*, Vol. 2, 1958, 256–271; quoted in A. Touraine *et al.*, *Workers' Attitudes to Technical Change*, O.E.C.D., 1965, 75.

111. K. Lewin, "Frontiers in Group Dynamics", *Human Relations*, Vol. 1, 1947, 5–41.

112. W. G. Bennis, "Post-Bureaucratic Leadership", *Trans-Action*, July–August 1969, 44.

113. T. Lester, "Geest Goes to Market", *Management Today*, April 1972, 84–89, 142–144.

114. J. Woodward, *Industrial Organization: Theory and Practice*, Oxford University Press, 1965; also J. Woodward, editor, *Industrial Organization: Behaviour and Control*, Oxford University Press, 1970.

115. C. Perrow, *Organizational Analysis: A Sociological View*, Tavistock, 1970.

116. A. K. Rice, *The Enterprise and Its Environment*, Tavistock, 1963.

117. J. Child, "Organizational Structure, Environment and Performance: The Role of Strategic Choice", *Sociology*, Vol. 6, 1972, 1–22.

118. J. Hage and M. Aiken, "Routine Technology, Social Structure and Organizational Goals", *Administrative Science Quarterly*, Vol. 14, 1969, 366–376.

119. E. L. Trist *et al.*, *Organizational Choice*, Tavistock, 1963; see also, E. J. Miller and A. K. Rice, *Systems of Organization*, Tavistock, 1967.

120. W. J. Paul and K. B. Robertson, *Job Enrichment and Employee Motivation*, Gower Press, 1970.

121. R. W. Revans, *New Society*, 2 January 1964.

122. P. M. Blau, "The Formal Theory of Differentiation in Organizations", *American Sociological Review*, Vol. 35, April 1970, 201–218.

123. J. C. Worthy, "Factors Influencing Employee Morale", *American Sociological Review*, Vol. 15, 1960.

124. L. W. Porter and E. E. Lawler, "The Effects of 'Tall' versus 'Flat' Organization Structures on Managerial Job Satisfaction", *Personnel Psychology*, Vol. 17, 1964.

125. B. Indik, "Some Effects of Organization Size on Member Attitudes and Behaviour", *Human Relations*, Vol. 16, 1963.

126. R. Heller, *The Naked Manager*, Barrie and Jenkins, 1972.

127. D. A. Schon, *Technology and Change*, Pergamon, 1967.

128. See R. W. Peterson, "New Venture Management in a Large Company", *Harvard Business Review*, Vol. 45 (3), May–June 1967, 68–76; also R. Brady, "Du Pont Gets its New Market Taped", *The Times Business News*, 8 January 1968.

129. J. W. Selden, division vice-president for 3M's New Products Commercial Development, quoted in R. W. Peterson, Ref. 128.

130. P. J. Sadler and B. A. Barry, *Organizational Development*, Longmans Green, 1970, 58.

131. P. N. Khandwalla, *Environment and the Organization Structure of Firms*, McGill University Faculty of Management Working Paper, 1970.

132. J. K. Galbraith, *The New Industrial State*, Hamish Hamilton, 1967.

133. D. S. Pugh *et al.*, "The Context of Organization Structures", *Administrative Science Quarterly*, Vol. 14, 1969, 91–114.

134. D. Thomas, "The Meaty Product of Scot", *Management Today*, March 1972, 83–89.

135. A. Fox, *Industrial Sociology and Industrial Relations*, Research Paper No. 3 for the Royal Commission on Trades Unions and Employers Associations, H.M.S.O., 1966.

136. D. Pym, "Effective Managerial Performance in Organizational Change", *Journal of Management Studies*, Vol. 3 (1), February 1966, 73–84.

137. M. L. Kohn, "Bureaucratic Man", *New Society*, 28 October 1971, 820–824. See also, M. L. Kohn, *Class and Conformity: A Study in Values*, Dorsey Press, 1969.

138. See R. K. Merton, "Bureaucratic Structure and Personality" in R. K. Merton, editor, *Reader in Bureaucracy*, Free Press, 1952.

139. J. Woodward, *Industrial Organisation: Theory and Practice*, Oxford University Press, 1965.
140. J. Martindell quoted in H. Koontz, editor, *Toward a Unified Theory of Management*, McGraw-Hill, 1966, 26.
141. R. Stewart, "The Computer Disillusion", *Management Today*, September 1967, 96–99.
142. T. J. Watson, Jr., "Creativity: A Major Business Challenge", *Columbia Journal of World Business*, Vol. 1 (1), Fall 1965, 32.
143. K. Lewin, "Frontiers in Group Dynamics", *Human Relations*, Vol. 1, 1947, 34.
144. L. Festinger *et al.*, *Theory and Experiment in Social Communication: Collected Papers*, Institute for Social Research, University of Michigan, 1950.
145. E. Ginzberg and E. W. Reilley, *Effecting Change in Large Organizations*, Columbia University Press, 1957.
146. W. D. Seymour, "Re-training for Technological Change", *Personnel Management*, December 1966, 183–190.
147. R. Heller, *The Naked Manager*, Barrie and Jenkins, 1972.
148. L. R. Sayles and G. Strauss, *Human Behaviour in Organisations*, Prentice-Hall, 1966, 318.
149. W. J. Dickson and F. J. Roethlisberger, *Counseling in an Organization*, Bailey Bros. and Swinfen, 1966.
150. L. Coch and J. R. P. French, Jr., "Overcoming Resistance to Change", *Human Relations*, Vol. 1, 1948, 512–532.
151. T. Lester, "Tightened Belts at B.E.A.", *Management Today*, February, 1972, 60–65, 126–130.
152. D. McGregor, *The Human Side of Enterprise*, McGraw-Hill, 1960, 125.
153. K. Davis, "The Case for Participative Management", *Business Horizons*, Vol. 6 (3), Fall 1963, 55–60.
154. D. McGregor, Ref. 152.
155. B. P. Smith, "Setting Management's Style", *Management Today*, May 1972, 105–108.
156. D. Cartwright and A. Zander, editors, *Group Dynamics: Research and Theory*, Tavistock, 1960, 182.
157. Quoted in N. R. F. Maier, *Psychology in Industry*, Houghton Mifflin, Boston, 1946, 264–266.
158. D. Thomas, "The Landscaped Office", *Management Today*, May 1967, 76–79, 142, 144.
159. P. Hill, *Towards a New Philosophy of Management*, Gower Press, 1971.
160. C. Argyris, "Today's Problems with Tomorrow's Organisations", *Journal of Management Studies*, Vol. 4 (1), February 1967, 53–54.
161. P. Lynch, "How to Bargain for Productivity", *Management Today*, May 1972, 117–128.
162. F. E. Emery and J. Marek, "Some Socio-Technical Aspects of Automation", *Human Relations*, Vol. 15 (1), February 1962, 17–25.
163. J. R. P. French, Jr., I. C. Ross, S. Kirby, J. R. Nelson, and P. Smyth, "Employee Participation in a Program of Industrial Change", *Personnel*, Vol. 35 (3), November–December 1958, 16–29.

164. E. C. Miller, *Objectives and Standards: An Approach to Planning and Control*, American Management Association, 1966, 38.
165. E. H. Schein, *Process Consultation: Its Role in Organization Development*, Addison-Wesley, 1969.
166. C. Argyris, *Intervention Theory and Method: A Behavioural Science View*, Addison-Wesley, 1970.
167. F. C. Mann, "Studying and Creating Change: A Means to Understanding Social Organizations", *Research in Industrial Human Relations*, C. M. Arensberg, editor, Harper, 1957.
168. F. Friedlander, "The Impact of Organizational Training Laboratories upon the Effectiveness and Interaction of On-Going Work Groups", *Personnel Psychology*, Vol. 20 (3), Autumn 1967, 289–309.
169. P. Spencer and C. Sofer, "Organizational Change and its Management", *Journal of Management Studies*, Vol. 1 (1), March, 1964, 41.
170. F. C. Mann and F. W. Neff, *Managing Major Change in Organizations*, Braun and Brumfield Inc., Michigan, 1961, quoted in Ref. 169.
171. T. Lupton, "The Practical Analysis of Change in Organizations", *Journal of Management Studies*, Vol. 2 (2), May 1965, 226.
172. F. E. Fiedler, *A Theory of Leadership Effectiveness*, McGraw-Hill, 1967, 255–260.
173. R. D. Laing, H. Phillipson, and A. R. Lee, "The Spiral of Perspectives", *New Society*, 10 November 1966, 713–716; see also, idem., *Interpersonal Perception*, Tavistock, 1966.
174. K. Davis, *Human Relations at Work*, McGraw-Hill, 1967, 155.
175. D. McGregor, *The Human Side of Enterprise*, McGraw-Hill, 1960, 223.
176. C. K. Ferguson, "Management Development in Unstructured Groups", *California Management Review*, Spring 1959, 66–72.
177. C. Argyris, "T-Groups for Organizational Effectiveness", *Harvard Business Review*, Vol. 42 (3), March–April 1964, 60–73.
178. D. McGregor, Ref. 175, p. 220.
179. C. Argyris, Ref. 177.
180. W. J. Reddin, "Training to a T", *Personnel Magazine*, Vol. 33 (325), August 1967, 28–30.
181. G. Edwards, "The Puzzle of AA", *New Society*, 28 May 1964, 10–11.
182. Apart from the research mentioned in this chapter, several evaluation studies are summarized in C. L. Cooper and I. L. Mangham, "T-Group Training: Before and After", *Journal of Management Studies*, Vol. 7 (2), May 1970, 224–239.
183. D. McGregor, *The Human Side of Enterprise*, McGraw-Hill, 1960.
184. D. Pugh, *T-Group Training*, F. P. G. Whitaker, editor, Blackwell, 1965.
185. M. B. Miles, "Changes During and Following Laboratory Training: A Clinical-Experimental Study", *Journal of Applied Behavioural Science*, Vol. 1 (3), 1965, 215–243.
186. D. R. Bunker, "Individual Application of Laboratory Training", *Journal of Applied Behavioural Science*, Vol. 1 (2), 1965, 131–148.
187. D. Moscow, "After the T-Group is Over", *New Society*, 29 December 1966.
188. J. B. Boyd and J. D. Ellis, "Findings of Research into Senior Management Seminars", Hydro-Electric Power Commission of Ontario, 1962.

189. C. Argyris, "Explorations in Interpersonnel Competence—II", *Journal of Applied Behavioural Science*, Vol. 1 (3), 1965, 225–269.
190. T. Lupton, "Organizational Change: 'Top-Down' or 'Bottom-Up' Management?", *Personnel Review*, Vol. 1 (1), Autumn 1971, 22–28.
191. N. O. Morse and E. Reimer, "The Experimental Change of a Major Organizational Variable", *Journal of Abnormal and Social Psychology*, Vol. 52, 1965, 120–129.
192. I. Mangham and C. L. Cooper, "The Impact of T-Groups on Managerial Behaviour", *Journal of Management Studies*, Vol. 6 (1), February 1969, 53–72.
193. P. B. Smith and T. F. Honour, "The Impact of Phase 1 Managerial Grid Training", *Journal of Management Studies*, Vol. 6 (3), October 1969, 318–330.
194. R. R. Blake *et al.*, "Breakthrough in Organization Development", *Harvard Business Review*, Vol. 42, 1964, 133–155; L. E. Greiner, "Antecedents of Planned Organization Change", *Journal of Applied Behavioural Science*, Vol. 3, 1967, 51–58.
195. E. Ginzberg and E. W. Reilley, *Effecting Change in Large Organizations*, Columbia University Press, 1957.
196. A. K. Rice, *The Enterprise and the Environment*, Tavistock, 1963, 276.
197. Larry E. Greiner, "Patterns of Organization Change", *Harvard Business Review*, Vol. 45 (3), May–June 1967, 119–130.
198. P. Ferris, "Shell After McKinsey", *Management Today*, May 1966, 98–103.
199. P. Selznick, *Leadership in Administration*, Row, Peterson, 1957, 108.
200. J. Thackray, "Comeback by American Can", *Management Today*, May 1967, 96–100.
201. P. M. Blau and W. R. Scott, *Formal Organizations*, Chandler Publishing Co., San Francisco, 1962.
202. A. W. Gouldner, *Patterns of Industrial Bureaucracy*, Routledge and Kegan Paul, 1955.
203. R. H. Guest, *Organizational Change*, Dorsey Press, Irwin, 1962.
204. A. W. Gouldner, Ref. 202, p. 38.
205. A. W. Gouldner, Ref. 202, p. 39.
206. A. W. Gouldner, Ref. 202, p. 46.
207. A. W. Gouldner, *Wildcat Strike*, Harper Torchbooks, 1965, 72.
208. Ref. 203, p. 22.
209. D. McGregor, *The Professional Manager*, McGraw-Hill, 1967, 58.
210. D. McGregor, *The Human Side of Enterprise*, McGraw-Hill, 1960.
211. *Ibid.*, p. 88.
212. R. R. Blake and J. S. Mouton, *The Managerial Grid*, Gulf Publishing Co., 1964.
213. R. Likert, *New Patterns of Management*, McGraw-Hill, 1961.
214. W. J. Reddin, "A 3-D Development in Management Style Theory", *Personnel Management*, March 1967.
215. *Ibid.*, p. 22.
216. A. W. Gouldner, *Patterns of Industrial Bureaucracy*, 39.
217. A. W. Gouldner, Ref. 216, p. 81.
218. A. W. Gouldner, Ref. 216, p. 71.

219. R. H. Guest, Ref. 203, p. 40.
220. R. H. Guest, "Managerial Succession in complex Organizations", *American Journal of Sociology*, Vol. 68, 1962–1963, 47–54.
221. A. W. Gouldner, Ref. 216, p. 72.
222. E. Fleishman, "Leadership Climate, Human Relations Training and Supervisory Behaviour", *Personnel Psychology*, Vol. 6, 1953.
223. R. H. Guest, Ref. 203, p. 42.
224. A. W. Gouldner, Ref. 207, p. 155.
225. A. W. Gouldner, Ref. 207, p. 158.
226. R. H. Guest, Ref. 203, p. 21.
227. P. Spencer and C. Sofer, "Organizational Change and its Management", *Journal of Management Studies*, Vol. 1 (1), March 1964, 44.
228. A. W. Gouldner, Ref. 202, p. 73.
229. J. A. C. Brown, *The Social Psychology of Industry*, Penguin Books, 1954, 55.
230. A. Judson, *A Manager's Guide to Making Changes*, John Wiley, 1966.
231. A. Willener, "The Worker and the Organizational System", in A. Touraine *et al.*, *Workers' Attitudes to Technical Change*, O.E.C.D., 1965, 61–64.
232. Quoted in A. Pettigrew, "Managing Under Stress", *Management Today*, April 1972, 99–102.
233. I. Barmash, *Welcome to Our Conglomerate—You're Fired!*, Weidenfeld and Nicolson, 1971.
234. L. E. Greiner, "Patterns of Organization Change", *Harvard Business Review*, Vol. 45 (3), May–June, 1967, 119–130.
235. A. K. Rice, *The Enterprise and its Environment*, Tavistock, 1963, 277.

Bibliography

J. M. Thomas and W. G. Bennis, editors, *Management of Change and Conflict: Selected Readings*, Penguin Books, 1972.

A. Judson, *A Manager's Guide to Making Changes*, John Wiley, 1966.

A. Touraine *et al.*, *Workers' Attitudes to Technical Change*, O.E.C.D., 1965.

J. K. Galbraith, *The New Industrial State*, Hamish Hamilton, 1967.

C. Argyris, *Integrating the Individual and the Organization*, John Wiley, 1964.

D. McGregor, *The Human Side of Enterprise*, McGraw-Hill, 1960.

R. Lippitt, J. Watson and B. Westley, *The Dynamics of Planned Change*, Harcourt, Brace and World, 1958.

G. W. Dalton, P. R. Lawrence and L. E. Greiner, editors, *Organizational Change and Development*, Richard D. Irwin, 1970.

G. W. Dalton, P. R. Lawrence and J. W. Lorsch, editors, *Organizational Structure and Design*, Richard D. Irwin, 1970.

H. A. Hornstein, B. B. Bunker, W. W. Burke, M. Gindes and R. J. Lewicki, editors, *Social Intervention: A Behavioural Science Approach*, Collier-Macmillan, 1971.

R. J. Hacon, editor, *Personal and Organization Effectiveness*, McGraw-Hill, 1972.

Index

169